DATE DUE

~~JA 1~~		
~~JA 28~~		
~~JE 11 '03~~		

DEMCO 38-296

AY, CUBA!

Books by Andrei Codrescu

Memoirs

Road Scholar
The Hole in the Flag: An Exile's Story of Return and Revolution
In America's Shoes
The Life and Times of an Involuntary Genius

Essays

Hail Babylon!
Zombification
The Muse Is Always Half-Dressed in New Orleans
The Disappearance of the Outside
Raised by Puppets Only to Be Killed by Research
A Craving for Swan

Poetry

Alien Candor
Belligerance
Comrade Past and Mister Present
Selected Poems: 1970–1980
Diapers on the Snow
Necrocorrida
For the Love of a Coat
The Lady Painter
The Marriage of Insult and Injury
A Mote Suite for Jan and Anselm
Grammar and Money
A Serious Morning
Secret Training
the, here, what, where
The History of the Growth of Heaven
License to Carry a Gun

Fiction

Messiah
The Blood Countess
Monsieur Teste in America and Other Instances of Realism
The Reptentance of Lorraine
Why I Can't Talk on the Telephone

AY, CUBA!

A SOCIO-EROTIC JOURNEY

Andrei Codrescu

Photographs by David Graham

St. Martin's Press New York

Parts of this book in slightly or substantially different forms were first broadcast on
National Public Radio's *All Things Considered* in January 1998. Other portions
appeared in different shapes in *Life* magazine, August 1998, and in *The New York
Times Sunday Magazine,* February 1, 1998.

Design by Maureen Troy

Library of Congress Cataloging-in-Publication Data

Codrescu, Andrei.
    Ay, Cuba! : a socio-erotic journey / Andrei
Codrescu ; photographs by David Graham.
        p.   cm.
    Includes bibliographical references.
    ISBN 0-312-19831-0
    1. Cuba—Description and travel.   2. Cuba—Social life and
customs—1959– 3. Codrescu, Andrei, 1946–   —Journeys—Cuba.
I. Graham, David, 1952– . II. Title.
F1765.3.C63   1999
972.9106'4—dc21   98-40545
                                                                    CIP

First Edition: February 1999

10 9 8 7 6 5 4 3 2 1

NOTE TO THE READER

The names used for the individuals identified as Jack, Yasmina, Lenin Gonzalez, Esmeralda Hernández Dawson, Bill Huxtable, and Dr. Sylvia are not those individuals' real names.

CONTENTS

LIST OF PHOTOGRAPHS

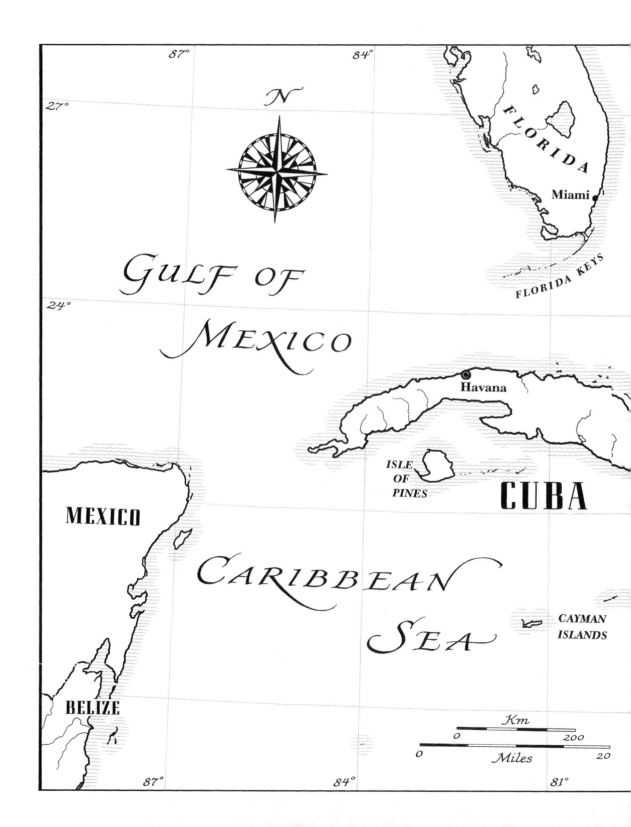

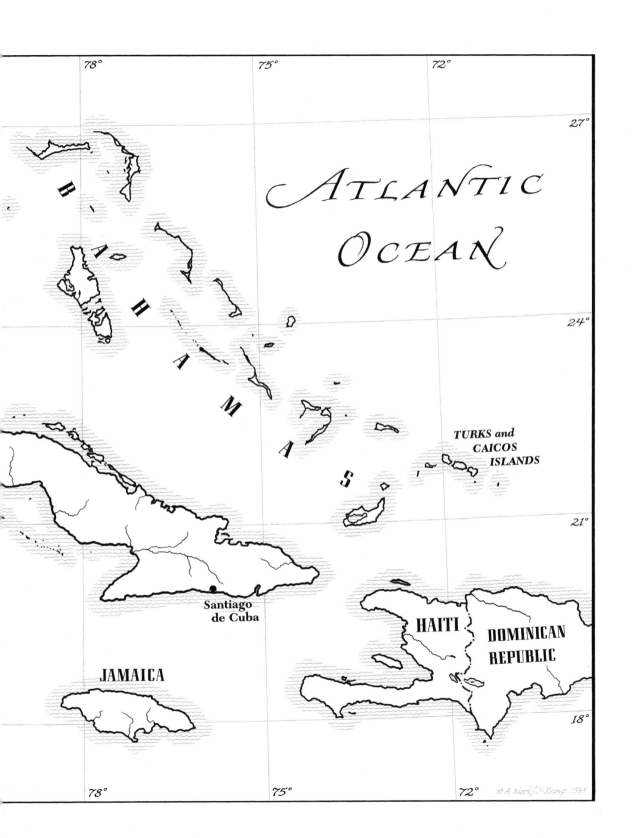

78°   75°   72°

27°

ATLANTIC

OCEAN

B

A

H

A

M

A

S

TURKS and
CAICOS
ISLANDS

24°

21°

Santiago
de Cuba

HAITI   DOMINICAN
          REPUBLIC

JAMAICA

18°

78°   75°   72°   ©A. Kivel / J. Kemp 1998

AY, CUBA!

PROLOGUE

The nicest sketches
drawn in our school tablets
always lead us to death.
And courage? What is it without a machine gun?

—*Heberto Padilla*, State of Siege[1]

One autumn day in Washington in 1997, when communism seemed to have prolapsed forever and the world looked in danger of becoming eternally boring, my friend Art Silverman said: "Would you like to go to Cuba?" Art is a senior producer at National Public Radio, and he firmly believes in stimulating my pseudo-journalistic persona. In 1989, he had contrived to send me to Romania with an NPR team to witness the momentous and violent finale of the last red domino in Europe. I filed a series of emotional reports from my homeland, reports that gained me an undeserved reputation for reportorial acuity. In fact, I had been overcome by sentiment returning to Romania after more than a quarter century in exile, and I had invested my observations with poetic feeling. The hard-boiled journalists fled Romania in droves when it became apparent, shortly after the execution of the dictator Nicolae Ceaușescu and his wife, Elena, that the shooting had (nearly) stopped. The typical hard-boiled journalist, seasoned in Lebanon, Somalia, and Iraq, had little use for a revolutionary operetta that had produced only a paltry harvest of bodies. For the most part, the collapse of Eastern European communism had been a bloodless, velvety affair; and that sort of thing, after decades of unrelenting cold war and arms races, was bound to be disappointing to the purveyors of frontline Hemingwayesque prose. That aftermath was better left to eggheads and poets, which accounted for my success as a "journalist."

What happened in 1989 in Romania and elsewhere in the fearsome "red empire" is still a mystery. The nuclear-tipped red menace, on the basis of which the West had built the mightiest war machine on earth, turned out to be some kind of sheep exhausted by having to wear its weighty wolf skin. I returned to Romania several times after "the revolution," and understood less and less of what had happened in 1989.

The only thing I did understand was that the people we'd called communists hadn't gone anywhere and were still pretty much the same, though they had changed some of their vocabulary for the sake of the times. It was now de rigueur to say "mister" instead of "comrade," but it was a new habit and the older folks kept slipping and saying "commister," or the native equivalent.

The mess that followed the execution of the Ceaușescus, the so-called "post-communist era," continued—and continues—to exhibit this split personality and has made it nearly impossible to gain any kind of "normality." The Romanians of the post-Ceaușescu age still have a long way to go before they can trust each other and go about their business without fear. The situation is compounded by the fact that the elite of the Communist Party and the secret police have adapted with great speed to the new conditions. In the age of "post-communism," different gangs are battling for power and money, using whatever it takes to sway the frightened populace, including fascist sloganeering, kitschy nationalism, gobs of nostalgia for paternal authoritarianism, and, of course, that perennial best-seller, anti-Semitism (without Jews). "Democracy" and "capitalism," fearful words at first, are now tossed about quite as casually as all the other words, because they are, after all, just words. What is actually going on is too feudal for Westerners to understand, but it is a legacy of what went on before, namely so-called socialism.

Perhaps an explanation for the quick collapse and the subsequent mess might be found in Cuba. Here is one of the last socialist countries in the world, a place nearing the end of its "great experiment," as Milan Kundera called it, a place where the communist ideology continues side by side with an encroaching and inevitable capitalism. Cuba is a laboratory of pre-post-communism and an ideal environment to study the dying beast while it is still (barely) breathing. Perhaps the nasty decomposition now taking place in Eastern Europe can be studied in Cuba because it is not yet total.

"Cuba?" I said. "Great idea."

I had only a vague idea why it was a great idea, but I knew why it was a great idea for Art. Winter was coming to Washington. Cuba is in the Caribbean. Weirdly enough, I don't have much interest in tropical paradises. Jamaica, the Bahamas, Tahiti—you can have them. There are certain parts of the world I simply don't care for. I am immensely attracted to Central and South America, the Mediterranean, the east coast of Africa. If I were an imperial writer like W. Somerset Maugham or D. H. Lawrence, for instance, two men who at a certain point in the mid-century divided the world between them to produce vast literary properties, I would leave the tropics to the competition. I have always loved the story of Maugham checking into the hotel in Oaxaca where Lawrence was staying and trying to invite Lawrence for breakfast, lunch, or dinner, or just coffee and conversation. After a month or so of being snubbed, Maugham gave up. He understood that Lawrence was laying claim to Mexico and telling Maugham to stick to the Indian sub-continent. I can barely imagine that sort of grandeur: Mexico is mine! Of course, when the sun set on the British Empire, only the writers were left to cover its missing limbs. But I have never felt ownership of any place, not even Romania, though I wish that those writers who keep insisting on writing about it would take an elementary course in the language.

The more I thought about Cuba, the more it made sense. In addition to explaining the mystery of the demise of communism, Cuba also held clues to the bewildering behavior of the victorious West. In the eight years since the collapse of the USSR there has been a mad scrambling in the United States and Europe for a new enemy to justify the maintenance of huge military machines. Eight years during which no adversary with the systemic authority of the red Ism arose. The specter of Islam, though skillfully painted in the most dreadful colors, failed to engage the public imagination to the same degree.* Ah, we missed the old commies! Not I personally, but Jesse Helms, the CIA, the Reagan Republicans, the Army, the Navy, and the Air Force.

Ah, but the Ism still twitched in China, Laos, Vietnam, North Korea—and Cuba. Of all these islands of commiedom, only Cuba engaged the full attention of our quickly thawing cold warriors. China was too big to mess with, because when you messed with China you messed with AT&T and Coca-Cola, which is to say with America. President Clinton, in one of the most astounding about-faces in American foreign policy, "decoupled" the issue of human rights from America's policy goals. The policy of human rights, which many commentators considered the winner of the cold war, was simply unhitched from the

---

*Poetic footnote: Between Ism and Islam lies a "la," a songy "la," which suggests that there is a "la-la land" quality about Islamic countries, something songy and dreamy that will not allow them to cohere into a hard whole.

wagon of our concerns. The moral authority on which the West based its claims of superiority over the authoritarian East was dropped like the proverbial hot potato, an act akin to dropping Faith or Grace from the Catholic canon. Without the bother of human rights, China could go right on filling its jails with dissidents, selling the human organs of executed convicts, and using slave laborers to produce cheap knockoffs of Cartier watches. With China protected by AT&T, North Korea on the brink of mass starvation, and other Asian communist countries too insignificant to bother with, only Cuba remained both a potent symbol and an unwavering target.

Cuba was in bad shape. After the loss of its Soviet patrons, the Cuban economy collapsed. But the Castro death watch was losing steam. A book called *Castro's Final Hour* by Andres Oppenheimer was already four years old. In late August 1997, a Miami television station reported that Castro had died, which caused the Maximum Leader to give one of his energetic mega-speeches and prove his ill-wishers wrong. "Good-bye to the imperialists' hopes," he said. "Pass what may pass, fall who may fall, die who may die."[2] The implication was that the Revolution would go on even if he died, but that he had no intention of dying.

The situation in Cuba at the end of 1997 resembled, at least superficially, from what I read, the situation in Romania in the eighties when austerity measures and poverty became unbearable. Facing economic disaster, Castro resorted to an unprecedented, out-of-character move that proved just how desperate the situation had become. He allowed the introduction of a rudimentary market economy, and the legalization of the dollar, which became quickly the only worthwhile currency on the island. Before this, owning dollars in Cuba was a crime. Many people went to prison for holding a small banknote. Now there are at least eight names for the dollar: *fula, guano, guaniquiqui, varo, peso, verde,* and, the official term for foreign exchange: *divisas.* European, Latin American, and Canadian companies were now invited to invest in joint ventures in Cuba. By the end of 1997, there were more than three hundred joint ventures in Cuba, mostly tourist resorts and hotels.[3] Cuban citizens were permitted to open small private businesses, such as hotels with a limited number of rooms, and private restaurants with no more than twelve tables. Some state land was turned over to tightly controlled cooperatives, and surplus produce was funneled to private markets. Expensive but previously unavailable goods, such as shoes, perfume, and sunglasses, became available in stores, for dollars only. Since the average monthly wage in Cuba was twelve dollars, these stores were clearly out of the reach of ordinary Cubans. These timid steps toward capitalism were taken in the hope of preventing a political collapse à la Romania, but also because Cuba's newest model for socialism, China, was doing the same.

There were also reports that Cuban musicians, artists, and writers, who had been censored, suppressed, and jailed, were being allowed more liberty. Cuban music, in particular, was becoming a valuable export and one that, Castro hoped, would not involve the export of the musicians as well as of the music, as had been the case in the past. In short, the regime was willing to do anything for hard currency (dollars) while maintaining some kind of ideological rectitude in a vacuum.

On January 21, 1998, the Pope visited Cuba. This event brought the island into the news and precipitated whatever processes were already taking place. In 1996, Castro had visited the Pope in the Vatican and invited him to Cuba, setting off shock waves among Cuban Catholics, who had been harassed and imprisoned throughout the life of the regime. There were very good reasons for Castro's pilgrimage to the Pope. After the loss of Soviet support, Cuba needed help to end the U.S. embargo. There were delicate political maneuvers that made possible the Pope's visit. The Cuban exiles in Miami were furious: they saw the papal visit as a Castro trick to shore up his dying dictatorship.

Conveniently, Castro, always quick to adapt, remembered that he had been raised Catholic, that his life had been saved by a Jesuit priest who didn't allow Batista's soldiers to shoot him, that his mother had been a believer. He had spent a week in the Convent of the Virgen de la Caridad del Cobre (Our Lady of Charity) near Santiago de Cuba in 1958, while his guerrillas cleared the way for his victorious march into Havana. While at the convent, he had been cared for and fed by a nun. In fact, going to see the Pope has been the way to save a flaming shithouse since the Middle Ages. Still, this particular Pope must have been especially odious to Castro because he had helped bring about the end of communism, first in Poland, then in the rest of Europe. He had been nearly killed by a KGB-inspired gunman in 1981. In this regard, at least, Castro, who had been the victim of numerous assassination attempts by the CIA, must have identified with the frail Pontiff. Fidel and John Paul had something else in common: the Pope was the authoritarian head of the Church, an absolute dictator who ruled by edict. On a personal level, dictators understand one another. During a visit to Spain the year before, King Juan Carlos had lectured Castro for an hour about the virtues of democracy and the prosperity of post-Franco Spain. Castro listened in absolute silence, then said: "Yes, but Franco had to die first."

The photograph of Castro shaking hands with the Pope at the Vatican became totemic. It was reproduced on T-shirts and posters. Putting an equals sign between the two figures was doubtlessly a propaganda coup for communist Cuba. This was the same Pope who'd upbraided the liberation theologists of Nicaragua and had checked some of the pro-revolutionary priests and nuns of Central America. In other Central and South American countries, the Catholic Church had close ties to Cuban-inspired guerrilla movements, but in Cuba believers had been persecuted for years. Open-air masses, a traditional Cuban way of worship, were forbidden. Catholic schools were—and still are—closed. Believers suffered discrimination in workplaces. For all that, the puritanical attitudes of the Church served Castro well whenever the urge to call for Revolutionary purity seized him. In the early 1970s the government campaign against homosexuals and artists had the blessing of the Cuban Church. Castro's problem with religion was not ideological: he simply needed to replace the worship of God with the worship of Fidel and socialism. The giant gatherings in the Plaza de la Revolución in the better days of the seventies, when Castro thundered for hours, were religious revivals, open-air masses. The theology of Castroism was built on a religious model: Fidel was the Father, Che Guevara the martyred Son, the fallen revolutionary heroes early martyrs of the Church. Che was the Christ of the Cuban Revolution. He had died young and had been pure in his faith. He was the key to Castro the Father's religion. The Cuban Revolution might not have survived if Che, instead of being longhaired and intensely romantic, had been as ugly as the Cuban Secret Service made him when they sent him to start another revolution in Bolivia. What if Che had been physically loathsome? And yet Che, for all his symbolic beauty, was everything Cubans were not. He was a fanatic who believed, above all, in reason, whereas Cubans have always been and remain passionate, musical, and mystical. They would rather dance than dialectify. In 1960, just after Eisenhower approved the CIA's raid on Cuba, "Most Cuban town dwellers were fanatically in favor of the regime, thinking Castro had 'the same ideas as Jesus Christ,' and were longing 'to kiss the beard of Fidel Castro.'"[4] But now it was 1996, and at least in Castro's view, the hand was proffered to the Pope in acknowledgment of a rival. For the Pope and everyone else, it was an admission of defeat.

The Pontiff's acceptance of Castro's invitation to visit Cuba was the beginning of a propaganda war that intensified as the date of the visit neared. The stalwart right-wingers were violently opposed to a planned cruise organized by the Archbishop of Miami for one thousand exiles who wanted to see the Pope. The Helms-Burton Act of 1996, which had been passed following the downing of two U.S. aircraft by the Cuban air force, strengthened Kennedy-era laws that forbade U.S. citizens to spend any money in Cuba. But the State Department was willing to relax Helms-Burton for the duration of the papal visit. In Cuba, the long-repressed Church was suddenly allowed to hold open-air masses, and the Bishop of Havana even appeared on television.

There were convulsions. There was an incident reminiscent of the good old days following the Bay of Pigs. A Salvadoran national, trained in the United States, bombed several tourist hotels and bars in Havana, including La Bodeguita, Hemingway's favorite haunt. The terrorist, the regime declared, was put up to it by *gusanos* ("worms"), Castro's name for Cuban exiles. An Italian businessman was killed in the blasts, which Cuba said were "terrorist activities . . . organised, supplied, and promoted from the United States."[5] In the past, such incidents led to huge (organized) demonstrations in support of the regime, which then turned into rum-soaked musical fiestas that made everyone forget their growling stomachs. But this time, there was no call for national jubilation. After his arrest, the Salvadoran disappeared from the news. In the long-ago seventies, mass demonstrations had stroked Castro's ego and whipped up patriotism and "Revolutionary spirit," but in the late nineties, the dictator was suddenly wary of crowds. Even the repatriation of Che Guevara's bones to Cuba in 1996 did not, despite the get-out-the-masses effort, draw more than a moderate-sized mob. Che's remains, retrieved after thirty years from a secret grave in Bolivia, were enshrined in a mausoleum in Santa Clara. But the fervent worship of Che had worn thin after years of official reverence. The last crowd to turn up in massive numbers had not been adoring. In 1980, more than 100,000 people stormed the Peruvian embassy in Havana, demanding to leave Cuba. The widespread protest led to the Mariel boatlift, which rid Castro of 137,000 people who hated him, including political prisoners, but also common criminals, insane people, and State Security agents sent to infiltrate the exile community in Miami. And then there was the matter of crowds in Eastern Europe, which had brought down the dictatorships there, an event barely reported in the Cuban press. But in 1997, the people of Cuba were in no mood to either celebrate or get angry. They were too busy starving.

"The idea," Silverman said, "is for us to get there *before* the Pope."

It made sense. The world's media armies would descend on Cuba with the Pope, leaving no stone unturned. Going ahead of the Pope gave us a shot at virgin minds.

Yes, I wanted to go to Cuba badly. Not out of nostalgia for state socialism, which organized my first nineteen years, and certainly not out of any desire to be "an undertaker of communism," as one of my non-fans uncharitably put it. I wanted to go to Cuba because I wanted to see for myself a decomposing ideology before all its elements transmuted into the noxious gases that gag Eastern Europe now: the secret police turned mafia, the ripoff of state property, the nationalism, xenophobia, fascism, savage capitalism, media kitsch, prostitution, and tragico-hilarious parliamentarianism. If all these elements were already visible *in nuce* in Cuba, then surely one could see how and why they so quickly metastasized in the ex-commie fiefdom.

Yes, but Cuba is different, everyone told me. Cuba is not a classical Soviet-style socialist country. Cuba is an *American* problem. Meaning, a *North* American problem. Cuba has been an obsession for the United States since the war with Spain in 1898, exactly a century ago. Cuba has been both a cheap and bountiful mistress and "a dagger in our back." The intensity of Cuban-American relations is that of estranged lovers. It has nothing to do with communism, socialism, or even capitalism. We are talking about *une affaire du coeur*. This little island ninety miles off the Florida coast has been constantly in our thoughts for over three centuries. Maybe longer. It had certainly been in *my* thoughts for at least three decades.

CUBA ON MY MIND

There are no frontiers in this struggle to the death. We cannot remain indifferent in the face of what occurs in any part of the world. A victory for any country against imperialism is our victory, just as any country's defeat is a defeat for us all.

**—Che Guevara in 1965,
addressing delegates from the Third World in Havana[6]**

On the first school day after New Year's, 1959, Comrade Papadopolou, our "discipline teacher" and chief communist ideologue at the Gheorghe Lazar Lyceum in Sibiu, Transylvania, came to class exultant, flushed like a long-distance runner and beaming with the good news that another country had joined the glorious socialist camp. Comrade Papadopolou, who wore the first miniskirt in Europe, was the progeny of Greek Communists exiled to Moscow. She had been educated there and sent to Romania to teach and to dazzle my young mind with the curvaceous length of her bare legs. She had been up all night, she told us, listening to the radio report of Fidel Castro's march on Havana. I celebrated with her, expressing my ardent enthusiasm for the Cuban revolution in a manner guaranteed, I hoped, to draw her attention to the fact that I was thirteen and capable already of glorious erections.

Two years later, in 1962, my erections had found several objects of requited interest, but I was still in love with my discipline teacher, and was not surprised when she called on me to be platoon leader for a series of militaristic exercises that involved my class. We were given wooden rifles with attached wooden bayonets and marched to a field outside of town, where we rushed some straw figures that had crudely lettered signs around their necks proclaiming them to be "Yankee Bandits." While the comrade explained that the Cuban Revolution and Cuba's workingpeople were under attack from American imperialism, an attack that might lead to world war, we dutifully plunged our teenage bayonets into the Yankee Bandits. When the crisis—which, unbeknownst to us, was called the Cuban missile crisis—was over, we were commended for our defense of socialism. Comrade Papadopolou even took the extra step of congratulating me in person when she asked me to stay after class. She sat next to me, the fleshy pulp of her naked thigh touching my trembling uniformed leg, and asked me if I had a girlfriend. I was so moved, I could barely shake my head no—which was a lie—and then mumbled that I had only done my duty. Her revolution was mine.

Many years later, in Detroit, Michigan, in 1966, I was newly arrived in the United States, living in an apartment building on the edge of the Wayne State University campus, trying to lead an exciting hippie life of drugs and sex in the midst of revolution. All my neighbors were radical protesters against the Vietnam War. *The Fifth Estate,* still the only continuously published anarchist newspaper in the United States, had its offices around the corner. So did a bloodthirsty literary-political journal called *Guerrilla,* which featured Che Guevara's face regularly on the cover. The editor of this journal talked me into driving with him from Detroit to New York in a "driveaway" Cadillac to distribute the newest issue at some radical festival in Central Park. A "driveaway" was a car belonging to a transferred executive who paid an agency to drive his car to his new residence. These agencies hired hippies to drive, knowing full well that only about half the cars would make it to their destination without dents, spills, or joint burns. Even so, it must have been worth it. Our Cadillac was jammed full of the journal depicting an angry Che Guevara with his fist raised in the air and a four-inch headline that screamed: "VIVA LA REVOLUCIÓN!" In Albany, New York, we ran out of gas, and realized that we had less than two dollars between us. Albany, the seat of the New York state government, was a hilly podunk town full of short-haired people who looked at us with undisguised hatred. We left the Caddy in front of an ominous-looking official building and went in search of countercultural types willing to buy a few newspapers. After some oblique inquiries we came up to a suburban garage where, behind the closed door, Albany's entire counterculture was jamming. The homelike feeling of electric guitar noise and pot smoke was comforting. We went in, showed our goods, and explained our predicament. Suddenly, a hirsute giant tried to bring a cheap guitar down over my head. I ducked just in time, but the editor wasn't so lucky. Another longhair got him in the shoulder with a baseball bat, crying all the while: *"Fucking commies!"* We got out of there in a hurry, chased by these strangely reactionary counterculturists. We would have never gotten out of Albany if one of the garage denizens, a closet radical, hadn't followed us, pressed five dollars into our hands, and whispered, "Get out of Albany. Che Guevara is the devil here."

A year later, on New York's Lower East Side, at the corner of Second Avenue and St. Mark's Place, I saw this young man again, panhandling. He had a red-starred beret on his head, and he looked for all the world like Che. Thousands, maybe tens of thousands of young men of the late sixties, early seventies, took on the Christ-like starved look of the romantic hero. Only the loss of their tresses in the next decade caused them to abandon their ideal. Certainly they didn't drop it because of the knowledge, current for two decades now, that Che Guevara had been an insane ideological maniac who fervently wished for a nuclear war during the Cuban missile crisis. In his biography of Che, Jon Lee Anderson writes:

> At the moment of maximum tension—after a Russian SAM (surface-to-air missile) brought down an American U-2 spyplane, killing its pilot—Fidel cabled Khrushchev, telling him he expected Moscow to launch its missiles *first* in the event of an American ground invasion; he and the Cuban people, he assured him, were ready to die fighting. Only a day later, Fidel learned that Khrushchev had made a deal with JFK behind his back—offering to pull the missiles in exchange for a promise not to invade Cuba and a withdrawal of U.S. Jupiter missiles from Turkey. Fidel was incredulous and furious that the deal was made behind his back, and reportedly smashed a mirror with his fist when he was told. Che tersely ordered his troops to sever his command post's communications line with the adjacent Soviet missile base, and raced off to Havana to see Fidel. . . . In an interview with Che a few weeks after the crisis, Sam Russell, a British correspondent for the socialist *Daily Worker*, found Guevara still fuming over the Soviet betrayal. Alternately puffing a cigar and taking blasts on his asthma inhaler, Guevara told Russell that if the missiles had been under Cuban control, they would have fired them off.[7]

This was the guy my erstwhile red-star-bereted contemporaries held up as a saint. I knew as little about Che as they did, but the few quotes I'd read sounded identical to the hogwash that had been poured in vast quantities over my adolescence by Communist Party fanatics.

My driveaway pal and I made it to the radical fest in Central Park and dumped a few thousand *Guerrillas* on the crowd. We were even greeted officially by some Black Panthers, who ran the show wearing

Che berets and rifles. I felt extremely fortunate to make it back to Detroit (by Greyhound) without further revolutionary episodes. My true intentions were, as I've said, far from revolutionary and I was amused, when I wasn't sickened, by the Leninist rhetoric of all the white middle-class Americans pretending otherwise. Even the Black Panthers, who may have had better reasons for playing revolutionary, had no idea what life was like in a commie paradise.

There were others, for whom the Revolution and Cuba were a full-time business. The most mysterious of these people was my upstairs neighbor, a statuesque, Indian-featured Peruvian woman who was rumored to be "a true Revolutionary," on an important mission. One day, while I was smoking a quiet joint with an overweight student named Millie whom I hoped to bed, a gunshot rang out and the ceiling over the bed started pouring down on us. I rushed up the stairs. The door flew open, and standing there in all her statuesque glory was Esmeralda Hernández Dawson, entirely naked, her nipples erect and angry. She explained that she had been cleaning her weapon when it went off by mistake, and invited me in for tea. Forgetting all about Millie, I sat down cross-legged on Esmeralda's floor while she brewed the tea. When she returned, still as naked as before, she put the teapot down on the floor—furniture was pretty counterrevolutionary back then—and, towering above me, she asked: "Can you help me look for crabs?" Her pubic hair was a luxuriant mass of black curls. It had been invaded by these sexually transmitted creatures, abundant then in our milieu, creatures she called "jewels on Venus." She explained, while I parted each strand and pulled off the many-legged "jewels," that the reason why they were thus called was that they caused a constant itch which, being scratched, gave rise to pleasure. Such pleasure-causing agents, while bothersome, were actually a gift of love, hence "jewels." I was less enthralled by her explanation than caught in the quandary of what to do with my mindless erection. Esmeralda solved this problem for me by asking me to massage her clitoris while she masturbated me. She talked the whole time, delivering herself of a political lecture on the Cuban Revolution. She had been to Cuba, she told me, where she had found an extraordinary people ready to die for socialism and Fidel. She had met Che Guevara and had shaken his hand. She gave me to believe that she had received her important mission from Che himself. I climaxed in her hand, the same one presumably shaken by Che, and the same one that had held the gun which had accidentally discharged. My encounter with Cuba and the Cuban Revolution seemed fated to a sexual context.

Esmeralda Hernández Dawson *was* a Revolutionary. Many years later, in 1977, under different circumstances, I found out that she was a major cocaine trafficker who bought weapons for the Peruvian guerrilla army Sendero Luminoso, a.k.a. the Shining Path. Whether she had received her mission from Che or not, she was an important link in the Cuban export of revolution. I discovered also that Esmeralda, dedicated to the Revolution though she was, had used a small part of her profits to acquire an apartment in Rome as retirement insurance. I don't know whether she ever got to use it, because she disappeared from my life that year. She may have gone to the mountains to fight with her comrades, been busted by the feds, or transferred to the Italian Red Brigades. Being a revolutionary was an international business for two decades, a mix of drug-dealing idealism, terrorism, and romance. The Cuban inspiration for this business continued long after some of the "liberation struggles" either degenerated into drug mafias or went off the ideological radar. The Shining Path, for instance, evolved into a bloodthirsty gang of fanatics who decapitated Indian peasants in front of their families.

Cuba, then, in my milieu of the late sixties until the mid-seventies, stood for everything good in the fight against Amerikan imperialism. There was no possibility of reasonable conversation on the subject. You were either for or against Cuba. The poet Lawrence Ferlinghetti, who committed some kind of lèse-majesté with a mild criticism of Cuba, ended up reviled as far as the bathroom walls at the Vesuvio Café in San Francisco, where a graffito proclaimed grimly: "Cuba sí Ferlinghetti no." Some of my radical contemporaries managed to visit the mother ship itself, with the Venceremos Brigade or as part of delegations of American youth to Havana. In Cuba they often met Fidel Castro, who exhorted them to fight before sending them into the fields to cut sugarcane. Some of them experienced the discomfort and indoctrination they received there with revolutionary stoicism and returned ever more determined to fight "the capitalist hydra," and ever more contemptuous of hedonist anarchist-liberals such as myself.

Having experienced firsthand the infinite boredom and constant low-grade terror of a post-Stalinist regime, I didn't shy away from disputing my revolutionary acquaintances' store of clichés, but to little effect. Yet, by virtue of many other generational interests, I found myself politically and socially on their side more often than not. I was against the war in Vietnam, because I did not see that particular war—as, in the end, most Americans did not—as a life-and-death contest between heathen communism and God-is-on-our-side democracy. We may look back on this era with superior hindsight, but there was a true radical spirit loose in the country because there were a lot of things wrong with this country. The Vietnam War, above all, filled us with despair. The assassinations of the Kennedy brothers, Martin Luther King, Jr., Black Panther activists, and others made us feel bereft. For some, the easy palliatives of communist ideology rushed in to fill the craters left behind by this despair. Our government, frozen in the cold war, waged an unrelenting war on the young for their opinions.

Margaret Randall, a young poet and activist, took up residence in Cuba in 1970, and filed dispatches like this one: "The *Rampa* is alive with Lenin . . . his presence in image and word, and the dictums are particularly apt for the daily struggle in Cuba now: that need for constant heroism in everyday work."[8] This sort of rhetoric was understood by most of us as simply that, rhetoric, but the specter of Leninism was a serious threat to the inevitably serious policing branches of our government. Such rhetoric was, in fact, a relief to the establishment, because its terms were familiar. The predominant tone of generational opposition outside such rhetoric was camp, clowning, and disrespect for hallowed symbols. The FBI would much rather deal with Marxism than with Groucho Marxism. And so would the Cubans, who, in 1967, expelled the poet Allen Ginsberg for chanting "Hare Krishna" in a Havana park and announcing loudly that Raúl Castro, Fidel's brother, was queer. Allen Ginsberg was infinitely more representative of the spirit of the youth revolt than the humorless likes of Margaret Randall.

Randall herself changed her mind very little. Eighteen years later, after returning to the United States from Cuba, a year after East European socialism went kerplunk, she wrote: "Cuba was essential; today it is *chic* to espouse long-distance views on that country's successes and failures, but it would be impossible here to overemphasize the impact made by the Cuban revolution on the lives of the generations of Latin Americans. Quite simply, David re-enacted his struggle with Goliath. A tiny island nation had shown the world that it was possible to stand up to the United States, reclaiming its identity and dignity."[9]

There is no arguing that Cuba did indeed reenact the struggle of David and Goliath at various times in its history, but 1990 was a far remove from 1962. We now knew that Castro's Russian bosses had kept the Cuban economy afloat with sugar subsidies; that the human rights situation on the island was deplorable; that Castro was a caudillo who maintained his grip on power with the aid of a vast security apparatus;

that many supporters of the Revolution had fled the country; that writers and artists who criticized the government were imprisoned; and that the romantic Che Guevara had nearly plunged the world into nuclear war with his "revolutionary intransigence."[10] When David was David one could view him as heroic, but when he became infatuated with Goliathism, insanity possessed him. Nonetheless, Randall's firmly set blinders are typical of many unrepentant left-wingers' views of Cuba. Just as many American Communists refused to see anything wrong with Stalin, so the Castrophiles ignore the evidence.

Ideology has an amazing way of warping the mind. In 1970, eleven Cuban fishermen disappeared—"kidnapped," Castro proclaimed, "by the CIA." When the fishermen returned, there was a huge demonstration in Havana to welcome them back. In the course of his hours-long speech condemning U.S. imperialism, Fidel admitted that the "ten-million-ton sugar harvest," for which Cubans had been drafted and worked half to death, had failed. Here are two descriptions of the same situation by two people on different sides of the fence:

> Out to the airport—Rancho Boyeros, outside Havana—the streets were already thick with people. . . . I've never seen so many people, but more impressive and harder to describe than the numbers I've never seen *such* people: the qualities of dignity, authenticity, and consciousness came through again and again like waves. . . . People who remembered it said, "This is second only to Fidel coming into Havana in January 1959!" . . . And then Fidel moved to the mike . . . spoke of responsibility and of international strategy . . . detailed the battle won by the Cuban people; their self-discipline, their courage, and their enormous will. . . . But he didn't leave it at that . . . and there was something else he had to tell the Cuban people: the ten million tons of sugar, which is the current superhuman struggle of a whole nation and an absolute challenge inside and outside Cuba, will not be achieved. [Margaret Randall, *Part of the Solution: Portrait of a Revolutionary*.[11]]

> The country had been devastated, thousands upon thousands of fruit trees and royal palms, even forests, had been felled in an attempt to produce those ten million tons of sugar. . . . The whole nation, completely ruined, was now the poorest province of the Soviet Union. . . . Of course, as usual, Castro refused to

admit his error, and tried to deflect attention from the failure of the sugar crop to other areas, such as his hatred of the United States, on which he placed the blame. A story was concocted about a group of fishermen kidnapped by CIA agents on some Caribbean island, and suddenly, the millions of people who had been cutting sugarcane for a year had to reassemble in Revolutionary Square or in front of what used to be the U.S. embassy in Havana, to protest the alleged kidnapping of the fishermen. It was grotesque to see those young men marching and yelling epithets at the United States. [Reinaldo Arenas, *Before Night Falls.*[12]]

The difference, of course, is that while Margaret Randall was an American, a touring Revolutionary who'd swallowed hook-line-and-sinker the mind-numbing sloganeering of the regime, Reinaldo Arenas felt its effects on his own skin, a Cuban skin.

The passing of time has certainly let much of the hot air out of the inflated rhetoric of sixties radicals, but many Americans who came of age then still have a soft spot for Cuba. For all the hard evidence, there is no arguing with sentiment. Despite what I now know about the fifties in Romania, I still have an irrational nostalgia for Stalinism, a time when nothing bad happened to children, no bad news was ever broadcast, and a puppy-warm lie spread over everything like a perfumed shroud over a maggoty corpse.

"WHY ARE *YOU* GOING TO CUBA?"

I begin to be free within those interchangeable limits:
the dawn will return.
islands are apparent worlds.

—Reina María Rodríguez, *The Islands*[13]

My mental baggage was laden with contradictory items. For several weeks before departure, I practiced slipping out a cool, understated "I'm going to Cuba" whenever somebody asked how I was. The guy at the front desk of my health club checked me in without looking up, mumbling a pro forma "Howreya?," and I iced him: "Going to Cuba." He looked up. "Isn't that Communiss?" "That's right," I said, gym bag over my shoulder, grim mouth, bored look that said, "That's the kind of thing I do. Hunt sharks."

Someone asked: "Isn't it illegal?" Well, yes, for most people. The laws of the United States forbid its citizens to spend money in Cuba. Which is tantamount to forbidding them to go there. For all that, 84,000 Americans visited Cuba, mostly illegally, in 1996, and the numbers keep going up. The Helms-Burton Act is hated by almost everyone, including U.S. customs agents who have to check travelers coming in from Mexico and the Bahamas and any of the many other countries that have normal relations with the island. I knew dozens of people who had been to Cuba, for various and multi-interesting reasons. Still, I was not going to Cuba illegally: I had a State Department Treasury visa, which is given to journalists and academics.

Most people whom I spoke with just reacted with envious glee. "Cuba! I always wanted to go to Cuba!" This was such a common reaction, I started asking why. "I don't know," somebody said. "It's just one of those things. I've been hearing about it all my life. I remember the Cuban missile crisis, when my whole third-grade class had to get under the desks. We were practicing for nuclear war."

One guy I told was a Kennedy conspiracy buff, well versed in the Cuban Theory, according to which Fidel Castro, tired of the CIA's attempts on his life, staged a successful counterattack. The conspiracy buff explained this, as well as the more familiar version according to which the CIA killed Kennedy because he had betrayed them at the Bay of Pigs. In the full version of this theory, the CIA collaborated with the Mafia in the assassination of the President because the Mafia, too, felt betrayed by the failure of the invasion. The Mafia was pissed about the loss of its casinos and whorehouses to Castro and had put all its faith in the Bay of Pigs invasion. Of course, the Mafia in those days had other reasons for hating the Kennedys. Attorney General Robert F. Kennedy had declared war on them. The FBI, too, had many reasons for hating the Kennedys and for bemoaning the loss of Cuba, chief among those reasons being certain delicate sexual transactions that high-ranking agents conducted on the island.

With Cuba seemingly at the epicenter of the Kennedy assassination, the island had been constantly present in the media for an entire quarter of a century. But in the past three years, since 1994, there'd been an increase of interest. One of my cigar-chomping friends explained it thus: "Cigars are in. Cubans make the best cigars. We want Cuban cigars." My friend pays $75 for a Cohiba cigar and $30 for a Romeo y Julieta, smuggled in from Canada. He cares nothing about politics. He knows that the Cohiba cigar was created especially for Fidel Castro, but this makes him crave it even more. My friend is twenty-eight years old and part of a new Gatsby-like generation of Americans dizzy with nineties affluence. For them, Castro merely guarantees the quality of their cigars.

A real estate agent I know has been going to Cuba regularly to buy property that belongs to the state. He buys it from Cuban lawyers in expectation of the post-Castro era of unbound capitalism. "That's crazy," I told him. "Would you buy the Brooklyn Bridge?" "If it was in Cuba!" he said. He also told me that the speculation is intense. Small, medium, and large vultures are circling the island, waiting for the old caudillo to croak. It was enough to make me feel sympathy for old Fidel.

I also told my old lefty friend Jerome that I was going. For Jerome, Cuba is still the unsullied socialist dream. He was quite distressed. "Why are *you* going to Cuba?" He knew that my background wasn't one to make me terribly sympathetic. That, at least, proved quite sensible, insofar as official Cuba goes.

And then there was Jack.

JACK

He saw himself a man ruled by dreams and all the water planets
of the emotions.

**—Himilce Novas,
*Mangos, Bananas, and Coconuts: A Cuban Love Story*** [14]

Jack's breakfast-and-lunch-only eatery in the Central Business District
in New Orleans has checkered tablecloths. The menu has forty different soups and sandwiches on it, including the rarely requested Cuban
sandwich: pork, tomatoes, and chicken. There is a wine list, but few
people drink wine at lunch anymore; it's strictly a mineral-water-and-
Fruitopia crowd. And let's not even talk about smoking, though Jack,
talking to me, after closing time, was puffing on a long Romeo y Julieta,
thirty bucks American, gotten for three in Santiago de Cuba. The tip
glowed an even quartz.

"I met her when she was fourteen and a half. . . . She'll be fifteen
this year. Here is her picture. . . ."

From a billfold stuffed with about $89,000 of credit, he pulled a
snapshot. It showed a girl in a green miniskirt, standing in water up
to her knees. She looked doe-tender, chocolate-hued, gazing with
uncertain flirtatiousness at the camera, her chest pressed forward to
emphasize what will one day surely be proud endowments. Around her
neck was a Pioneer neckerchief, testifying to her schoolgirl status and
socialism.

"I started going to Cuba in '93. It was unbelievable. I had one girl
in the morning, one in the afternoon, and one at night. . . . At this fiesta
in Santiago I had one waiting outside by the rum truck and I was boom-
booming by the wall this other girl I just met. . . . But then Yasmina
showed up with some high school friends. I told them all, no more, I
met the one."

Jack had met Yasmina in Santiago de Cuba, outside a salsa bar
called Casa de las Jovenes, a state-run institution, one among hundreds
in Cuba that provide circuses for the masses.

"You have to be careful," Jack advised, "when you pick a girl,
because once you pick her, she's yours. She won't move from your side,
she'll stay the night, whatever."

Yasmina wanted to stay the night with Jack, but Cuban girls aren't allowed in tourist hotels. Instead, they went to the all-night Club 300, where they swayed the night away and saw the pink dawn rise over the cathedral in Parque Cespedes. By dawn, Jack had found love. Never, to hear him explain, had he been lowered into such a furnace of girlish passion and exclusive attention. He asked Yasmina to go to the beach with him for the weekend.

Jack, fifty-two, with a ponytail and a silver-dollar-sized bald spot, twenty pounds overweight, twice divorced, a restaurateur and a member of the Rotary, bought a red rose from a tired flower girl dozing on a park bench.

"You'll have to ask my parents," Yasmina said.

Hand in hand, the two of them, he thirty-seven years her senior, walked the two kilometers from Parque Cespedes to a *solare* at the edge of the old city, and found Yasmina's mother, her grandmother, her four sisters, and her four little brothers still sleeping. The *solare* was a seventeenth-century building, recast for the living needs of large families into small cubicles with long dark corridors. A pig was tied to a crumbling wall just outside the low entrance covered by a frayed yellow curtain. The mother gave her permission.

For the next three days, Jack and Yasmina were lost to the world, spiraling down a transracial, transcultural, apolitical vortex that cared nothing about the embargo, dollars, or "the Bearded One." There were no reminders of these, in any case. Images of the Bearded One, to whom no one in Cuba refers by name, were absent. Only the huge mural of Che Guevara, the martyred son, looming over their $5-a-night *paladar*, reminded them now and then of "reality."[15] It was "reality" between quotation marks anyway, because Che's romantic image, detached from any political context, meshed only too well with the huge Caribbean moon and the coral reef in the crystal-clear water. Images of Che, like the "Che Song," with its "Querido Comandante Guevara / La transparencia de su presencia," wafting at obligatory intervals from a distant band, were meant as tourist enhancements—a little edge on the salsa, an extra slice of lemon in the Cuba Libres.

Jack spoke no Spanish, and Yasmina spoke no English. They lay on the beach teaching each other the rudimentary language of *amor*.

"She'd say something to me," Jack explained, still drunk with that now-distant moment, "and then she'd get mad at me for not understanding. I would pretend to be mad at her and then we'd laugh, and kiss."

When they returned from paradise, Jack was determined to make Yasmina his, and to prevent her from becoming a *jinetera*, or even a prostitute. To that end, he began sending her $100 a month through a Canadian bank. They speak on the telephone every week, which isn't easy, because Yasmina's family doesn't have a telephone. The closest telephone is at her uncle's two streets away. But every Friday, at a predetermined time, the two lovers who don't speak each other's language coo in the international tongue of passion and assure each other of their fidelity.

"I always say to her," Jack confessed with a grin, "*'Hasta la victoria siempre.'*"

That slogan, along with Che Guevara's picture, was the most visible sign of the Revolution in Cuba, according to Jack, and the victory it meant was victory for socialism, of course, but there you have it: *Amor vincit omnia.*

Jack gave me a package of clothes and an envelope stuffed with the photographs he took last time in Cuba, to take to Yasmina.

Santiago de Cuba, Cuba's second largest city, is in Oriente province, at the other end of the island from Havana. It is the heart of Afro-Cuba: the sun is hotter here; the people are darker, and, everyone believes, more passionate.

Jack assigned grave importance to the Pope's visit. "Maybe the embargo will come down," he said, "and I can live legally in Cuba, or bring her here." He'd been looking for a house to buy, just in case the Pope ended communism on the island. A permanent resident of Cuba married to a native can buy a house in her name. Jack was in love, but about marriage . . . well, he'd been around the block twice.

Jack gave me other useful counsel, and tips. He told me what to take with me, and that every guy in Cuba is named Jorge. "Shout it on the street," said Jack, "and twenty guys turn around." Alas. I didn't meet a single guy named Jorge.

WAL-MART

No consummation exists without being from some long
    previous consummation, and that from some other,
Without the farthest conceivable one coming a bit nearer
    the beginning than any.

—Walt Whitman, *Song of Prudence*[16]

According to Jack and to the real estate agent, the most sought-after items in Cuba, and the best presents, were soap, aspirin, and baseball caps. "But don't think for a minute," Jack warned, "that Cubans are dirty. They are the cleanest people in the world." But they did have headaches, and medicines were unavailable as a result of the U.S. embargo. (Most medicines are U.S. patented.) And they were crazy about baseball. Next in importance were clothes, particularly T-shirts with American business logos on them. Wearing them was a gesture of defiance by young Cubans. These items were not much different in desirability from the things I took to Romania in 1989. In fact, almost everything available in my corner drugstore in New Orleans would have made any Romanian of that era deliriously happy.

For my Cuba shopping I went to Wal-Mart. Now, Wal-Mart overwhelms me in normal circumstances. I am but a lost child when it comes to the immense variety of objects this cornucopia contains. I could live for years, unnoticed, inside Wal-Mart, eating out of cans and riding around in sleek lawn mowers. I could change clothes every day. I could create a new living space every few hours with new curtains, new furniture, and new plants. I could listen to music, though only the discounted variety, and read cheap but entertaining books. In the materially poor universe I grew up in, Wal-Mart would have been our utopia's fulfillment. What Karl Marx described as "communism" was Wal-Mart. What I wanted to do was tow the whole store to Cuba. Then I would set up shop at some intersection in Havana and distribute everything. I bet the throng would be bigger than the one for Fidel's biggest (and longest) speech. The irony, of course, was that starved Cubans would find Wal-Mart heaven, while bored Americans are constantly in search of spiritual nourishment. The problem with communism is that it started at the wrong end: instead of promising people material fulfillment at the end of the journey, it should have stuffed them at the beginning.

I bought T-shirts that said "Valvoline," "Tennis Academy," "Harley-Davidson," "Surf USA," and "Star Wars," and baseball caps that said "Yankees," "Pirates," and, best of all, "Marlins." The Most Valuable Player of 1997 was Livan Hernández, the Cuban pitcher for the Florida Marlins, winners of the World Series. Livan Hernández was a defector from Cuba who had played in the Cuban National League. This was a personal affront to Fidel Castro, who prided himself in the excellence of Cuban baseball and had almost pitched his way into the

U.S. major leagues in 1956.[17] Fidel had struck out Tommy Lasorda in an exhibition game attended by scouts from the Washington Senators in the days before they became the Twins. Livan's defection so rankled the dictator, he forbade Cubans to watch the World Series and blocked the broadcast. The entire nation went into a frenzy of improvisation, rigging wires from every rooftop to try to catch the games. The tourist hotels were full of Cuban guests watching the unjammed televisions. Among these guests, watching with friends from CNN, was Livan's brother, Orlando "El Duque" Hernández, Cuba's best pitcher, whom Fidel Castro had banned from baseball for life because of his brother's defection.

Next, I bought soap—six four-packs of Ivory soap, and some scented soaps in crinkly wrappers. I also filled the shopping cart with aspirin, cough medicine, decongestants, antidiarrheals, cold medicines, anti-fungal creams, and nearly everything else that could be had without a prescription. Of course, the greatest need must have been for antibi-otics, but I couldn't get those sans script. The cough syrup was for a high-ranking Cuban official whose telephone number I'd gotten from a Miami architect. When I asked the architect what kind of gift was appropriate for such a high-ranking person in gratitude for granting me an interview, he said, "Cough syrup," and explained that during his last visit the official had been very specific about this.

I bought several dozen pencils with baseball team logos on them to hand to kids on the street, though my guidebook said not to, blaming tourists for the existence of "beggars": "The beggars are a direct effect of tourism caused by the foolishness of previous visitors who amused themselves by handing out money, soap, pens, candies, chewing gum and other things to people on the street."[18] Now there is a novel way to create beggars: hand out chewing gum. This is advice akin to the zoo's "Don't feed the animals." The only difference is that the zoo does feed the animals. My guidebook, while not lacking in good information, was generally partial to that sort of logic. The "human rights situation" in Cuba, for instance, was "good . . . compared to Colombia, Peru, Brazil, Guatemala, and Venezuela." The book stopped short of blaming pam-phlets brought in by tourists for the existence of political prisoners, however.

I also bought candy, chocolates, and cigarette lighters. If things were at all like they'd been in Romania, lighters were at a premium. In Romania, people made disposable Bics into refillables by affixing a screw to the bottom. On my way out, I saw a sale on stockings, and bought several dozen pairs of sheer stockings that, I imagined, would cause great delight among the women of Cuba. But when I told Jack about the stockings, he laughed: "Forget it. Cuban girls and women have such beautiful, smooth legs, they don't need them." I think this, more than anything else, reflected Jack's wishes and desires. I have yet to meet a woman who disdains sheer silk.

Having filled two suitcases with an infinitesimal portion of Wal-Mart, I barely had room for my essentials, but then I travel light. After years of shlepping bags through airports, I carry only the indispensable, plus binoculars, mini tape recorder, and cheap camera. When my mother and I left Romania we were allowed only one suitcase per person. I couldn't take out any of my writings, and my mother, who was a photographer, couldn't take any of her photographs. But our suitcases bulged nonetheless, with clothes and shoes, which turned out to be worthless in the West where such things flowed like rivers from stores to garbage dumps after barely touching the people who owned them. Now I was going to Cuba, however, with two bulging suitcases that seemed to me in some logical but perverse way to be the same ones I'd gotten away with in that long-ago year 1965. When I had first returned to Romania, at the end of December 1989, communism had expired, so it made sense that if I returned to a communist country in 1997 I would be lugging the same weight. What sense does this make? I'll tell you. It is my firm belief that all the countries where the culture of Soviet-style socialism "flourished" are exactly the same. They have more in common with each other than with their nonsocialist neighbors, even if the neighbors speak the same language. All these countries are but one: Socialist Camp Land.

Was that crazy? Doubtlessly, I would find out.

ART AND DAVID

Then said Pantagruel, Come, my lads, let us begone, we have stayed here too long about our victuals; for very seldom doth it fall out, that the greatest eaters do the most martial exploits. There is no shadow like that of flying colors, no smoke like that of horses, no clattering like that of armor. At this Epistemon began to smile, and said, There is no shadow like that of the kitchen, no smoke like that of pastries, and clattering like that of goblets. Unto which answered Panurge,

There is no shadow like that of curtains, no smoke like that of women's breasts, and no clattering like that of ballocks.

—François Rabelais,
Gargantua and Pantagruel[19]

I met up with Art Silverman in Washington. He was officially the producer of the series of reports I'd contracted to do for National Public Radio. I say "officially," because somewhere in his mind he had conceived of the idea—inconceivable, if you know the NPR folk—that he might be taking some kind of vacation. I try to encourage this sort of thing as much as I can, because I know from experience that Art's idea of a vacation is to work only ten hours a day instead of his usual fourteen. Once, Art and I were in Seattle doing a piece on "cyberspace," and he reassured me that our light schedule would permit us to do lots of "fun" things. We ended up interviewing up to six (exhausting) cyberspace luminaries a day, in addition to experimenting with virtual realities—being shot, for instance, with death rays by violent sportsmen of the apocalypse—and having "fun" lunches with eggheads who liked to scribble math formulas on the tablecloth. If these lunches were Art's ideas of fun, his ideas of sin were downright shocking. Twice in Seattle he allowed himself a beer. And now we were going to Cuba, a place that fun-wise is to Seattle what samba is to the minuet.

Art had packed some serious suntan lotion, so I knew that, theoretically, we might be going to the beach. He also brought two or three tape recorders, lots of microphones, tapes, and various gadgets. In other words, "nothing at all," as he put it. I could tell by the way he had everything ready that taping would begin as soon as we left American soil.

The third member of our group, David Graham, was going to meet us at Nassau Airport in the Bahamas, our gateway to Cuba. He was flying in from Philadelphia with his cameras and other photo gear. I had also worked with David, and I knew that *his* idea of fun was much closer to Art's than mine. A relentless worker, he photographed whether he had his camera ready or not. He always scanned, squinted, took in the sights, put his hand out to gauge a picture.

With Art and David "having fun," I was guaranteed to end up an overworked wretch. But I have my ways. I decided long ago that, when surrounded by workaholics, I would resort to the two classical tactics of the poet under pressure: corrupt them and, if that doesn't work, disappear. I was ready to implement both.

We flew to Miami, changed planes, and flew to Nassau. On the plane, Art consulted a bulging folder containing clippings about Cuba and the upcoming visit of the Pope. He also had with him the galleys of a forthcoming tome-ette, which I ended up skimming and leaving behind in disgust. It was the saga of some middle-aged New Yorker who'd gone to Cuba full of smart-ass bravado and had had quite a few interesting adventures which he'd been incapable of understanding. Or describing. Every chapterette ended with an implied sexual encounter that terminated abruptly like a window shade dropping in a forties movie long shot. His blithe Yankee-ness was unmarred by either knowledge of the place or affection for it.

For the next hour, I thought undisturbed about what we were about to do. We were going to a poverty-stricken land of people who had done their utmost to prosper but could not. They surely had, as we had in Romania, a great many highly educated people, fine artists, writers, and musicians. Cuba was not sunk in ignorance: its professionals had gone all over the world to help third-world countries, mostly with revolutions, but also with medicine, agriculture, engineering. Cuba had an astounding number of doctors per capita, if the statistics were right. Cuba hosted congresses, academic conferences, film festivals.

In fact, we were—officially—going to the Havana Film Festival. This had come about because Art, wanting to give an extra thrill to our foray, decided that we should go undercover. Instead of going to Cuba as journalists, which is what we were, we were going to pretend that we were film professors going to view this year's entries in the festival. Originally, he'd wanted us to go illegally, like everyone else, but I'd nixed the idea. I've had too many doings with the bureaucrats of this planet to risk arousing their suspicion for nothing. Doing something like that gratuitously is like running for exercise: it's stupid. You should run when somebody chases you. I had no problem with being a film professor going to a film festival because I am a professor and I did intend to see a film or two. The Havana Film Festival was quite well respected as a showcase of Spanish-language cinema.

As we were landing in the Bahamas, I noticed that almost everyone around me was Hispanic. The sounds of Spanish floated throughout the plane, as did laughter. From the minute we had embarked in Miami, we had entered another world, one that was already louder, more spontaneous, and looser. Of course, most of the passengers were island-bound out of Nassau, so they were naturally happier, whether they were going home or on vacation. I wondered how many of my fellow passengers were going to Cuba. I couldn't tell, but I guessed not many. These folk were too cheerful. Travelers to and from commie lands are not, as a rule, cheerful. The Romanians of my era were downright grim. They cried when they got out (from happiness), and cried when they flew back in (from anxiety). I did notice two serious young women with severe shoulder-length haircuts and round Trotsky glasses who, doubtless, were going to Havana.

IN TRANSIT

Items one cannot bring into Cuba include narcotics, explosives, motorized vehicles, obscene publications, and pre-recorded video cassettes. The import of firearms, ammunition, weapons, telecommunications equipment, flora and fauna specimens, live animals, biological or pharmaceutical goods of animal origin, and unprocessed food (including all fresh fruit, meat, or vegetables) is restricted, so check beforehand.

—**David Stanley,**
   Cuba: A Travel Survival Kit[20]

There was a mild narcotic in the Bahamas air. The Caribbean puts forth sleep-inducing blooms. There were clusters of purple flowers outside. I couldn't glance at them without feeling my eyes closing. Even in Florida, where the coastline is thick with condos and luxury boats, the mild air induces dreaminess. Julio Hernández Max, a Cuban poet, wrote about the air of the Caribbean: "The invisible seeds of oily tropical blooms stick to you. / If you fall asleep on the beach, you wake up with flowers growing in your damp hollows."[21] I lived in places so humid moss grew from me, but never flowers. The idea of becoming a living greenhouse was so amusing that I began to add imaginary blooms to the people in the waiting room. Unbeknownst to himself, Art had a tall stalk ending in a violet bloom jutting out of the top of his head. The Trotsky girls sprouted lilac around their breasts. I gave the Cubans those thick tubular banana-tree blooms on each shoulder.

The Nassau International Airport was steeped in sea salt, fish, sweat, airplane fuel, and cheap cologne, and it oozed honey-thick tropical laziness from every pore. Perhaps it was the word "international" that had fooled me, or my idea of the Bahamas being some kind of wealthy Brit enclave, but the airport was nothing of the sort. Everybody was either snoring or nodding in an intense postcolonial reverie. A vast, gold-braided policeman in khaki shorts and British helmet was gawking with enormous glazed orbs at the legs of a plump stewardess, who was sprawled sleeping on a yellow bucket seat. Her high-heeled black pumps sat in the next chair like dugout canoes.

We looked around for David, who hadn't yet showed up, and wondered if we'd end up going to Cuba by ourselves. Art likes taking pictures, so I think that he may have been hoping.

While we were waiting in line to have our tickets stamped, an airline agent approached. "Do you need tickets for Cuba?" she asked everyone in line. The girls with Trotsky glasses bought round-trip tickets. So that's how it worked for U.S. citizens: in Nassau or Cancún or anywhere in the world with flights to Cuba, one can simply buy tickets. In Nassau, they approach you. The transaction did have a hint of furtiveness about it, although it was legal. There was a bit of defiance as one of the young women held out her money. She waved it a bit toward her companion and smiled thinly. Screw Helms-Burton, her smile said. Her friend smiled back: Make that a double.

We had some fried fish and yellow rice in the small cafeteria and read *The Bahamian News*. According to the paper, a sailboat had been stolen. Her Majesty's Court was taking up some property dispute involving eight feet of beach. The British soccer team was going to Holland. The tide was high. The weather forecast: sunny, in the mideighties. Two men seated at a nearby table argued something in Creole. Now and then I would make out a word or two: "belongame," "not likely mahn."

There was still no sight of David. Our flight was in one hour, but there were no planes in the cloudless sky. The passengers dozed on huge suitcases and boxes. A magic wand had passed over the Nassau International Airport. The only sound was the whirring of ceiling fans sucking in humid ocean air, and the clunk of chicken bones falling on plates.

I wandered over to a store called Nature's Gifts, which sold mostly detergents. The vendor was asleep behind the cash register. To the third world, detergent must be a kind of nature. I thought lovingly of all the cakes of soap I was ready to bestow on the Cuban nation. Normally, soap would have been the last thing I would have thought of. When I was growing up we took baths only once a week, on Saturday, which is what most Europeans do, and never worried about soap. We had these black cakes of pig fat, ashes, and lye that we scoured our skin and hair with, and we were clean as whistles. We knew what dirty was: peasants and Gypsies. We city kids knew for a fact that peasants were a strong-smelling bunch who slept with their animals and were redolent of wet wool, cheese, and garlic. As for Gypsies, it was rumored that they had a kind of filth religion that put off the *gaje*, though I wasn't put off in the least when it came to assiduously pursuing Gypsy girls, whose filth was heady and intoxicating. On Romanian trains I had smelled all classes of people and I liked them, even the sweatiest ones. I love the ruddy aroma of the Great Unwashed. America was obsessively clean; people rubbed themselves raw with cleansers. One of my Romanian friends who went bald a year after emigrating to the United States told me that he was sure that shampoo had made his hair fall out. I now use a shampoo whose slogan says it's "An American Attitude for Hair™," and I always wonder what kind of attitude this is, exactly. Americans have pretty violent attitudes about hair. In the sixties they killed each other over hair. Having just the right attitude about hair is difficult.

As I considered this profound thought, David finally showed up. He is a handsome fellow, with a full head of hair and a classic American face—looks a bit like the young Jack Kerouac. Now we were three. Three musketeers going undercover to the Havana Film Festival. David was excited. He'd never been to a Communist country before, he said. Art and I took in this confession with barely disguised superiority. I grew up in one, and Art had been to China, Vietnam, and Mongolia.

"Never been to a communist country?" I exclaimed. "Boy, are you in for the surprise of your life! They have no malls! There are no advertisements! Men carry hammers and ride tractors! Women carry sickles and ride combines! At night, when they meet, they put their hammers and sickles together and sing communist songs!" I really got going. This was going to be good. A Yankee in Stalin's court. We were going to have fun.

The three women manning the security gate were eating fried chicken, fish, and yellow rice, oblivious to the gaggle of passengers bunched before the checkpoint. When the chicken, fish, and every grain of rice were carefully masticated and disposed of, they stirred with evident regret, set the conveyor belt in motion, and began pulling us in. From their lack of interest in our electronics, I'd say that the Nassau International Airport rates on a par with, say, Lagos's security alertness. If you are planning to smuggle anything, do it after lunch in a tropical country.

When we reached the other side, I saw why nobody was in a hurry. The only airplane on the tarmac was the one David had come in, a Delta jet. I asked the man behind the coffee counter where the plane was. He shrugged. "Air Cubana . . . maybe two hours late." There was nothing to do but wait, which in the gentle Caribbean breeze, seemed almost like fate. It wasn't easy to fathom, but somewhere in this somnolent dolce far niente air there were demons that made history.

"These islands were made for sleeping," I told Art, who looked far from awake himself.

"Unless there's a hurricane." Art had something there. History was like hurricanes around here. Everything quiet, then *whammo.*

"Yeah," David said, "sleep on the beach in Cuba."

"In Cuba you can't sleep," I said. "They shine the light in your eyes all night. That's if there is electricity. If there isn't, they shine their flashlights."

And if the batteries are dead, you read by the light of rats' eyes. But I only thought this. I wasn't yet ready to tell David the whole truth.

We settled in to wait in the lounge at Departure Gate "A," which looked almost normal, with its metal bucket seats and "No Smoking" signs. I scanned the passengers: a suburban-looking American couple with kids; a guy in shorts reading the sports section of *USA Today;* two blond women absorbed by the obligatory airplane literature of Tom Clancy and John Grisham; a black man with salt-and-pepper beard and pseudomilitary cap, reading *How to Be Jamaican,* an illustrated book. These were the Jamaica-bound passengers. But then I noticed a woman reading a large-print leather-bound Bible and mouthing the words. Her seatmate, a man, was deep in a paperback called *The Bondage Breaker,* which I surmised was about religion, not S&M. I moved into the seat next to them.

"Excuse me," I asked the man, "are you going to Cuba?"

He admitted that he was, with a wide Texas accent and a smile. His name was Bill Huxley. He squeezed my hand hard in his large palm. Sleek black hair rose from his head in a small pompadour like young Elvis's. There was glistening pomade in it.

"Your first time?"

"Fifteenth," he said.

Well, well.

"I'm a sports evangelist."

I asked him what a sports evangelist was.

"We preach the Word to stars of the sports world who are models for youth so that they in turn can teach the Word."

"Have you made any inroads?"

Bill Huxley shook his head. "Not yet. But we take medicines to Cuba, help people out, pray and hope. To be honest, I enjoy the Cuban people even if they don't quite know what to make of us." Bill Huxley was a persistent and humble evangelist.

After 1989, Eastern Europe and Russia were overrun by missionaries of every stripe, from Baptists to Scientologists. The ex-commie fiefdom became a vast and fertile battleground for souls. The competition among those intent on saving the shriveled souls of atheists was fierce. One after another, God's colonialist grouplets planted their flags in the virgin real estate of ex-Commie souls, only to be shocked time after time at the scant results. It is true that, for a time, in Romania, an unusually large number of provincial engineers and young textile-mill workers conceived a great love for the God of the Seventh-Day Adventists. But then, it turned out that they had misread the promise of the church: not *everyone* who converted could emigrate to America. There was still the matter of U.S. immigration laws. God had no pull with the INS because the INS, as everyone knows, is godless. Here was something the new converts found very hard to understand: how was it possible that America's gods and America's institutions operated under different authorities? Under communism, God, a.k.a. the Party Secretary, operated all the institutions. It was simple. Many of the new converts became very disgusted with the impotence of religion after this, and reconverted to communism, under which things were simple. Not everyone reconverted: some of the evangelicals handed out food and medicine, and many of the orientally inspired cults gave out pretty colored books free of charge. The weak governments of the shaky new democracies behind the shredded Iron Curtain did not like this invasion of soul snatchers, but there was little they could do. In Russia, after persistent carping by the Russian Orthodox Church, the majority religion, some threatening noises were directed at the armies of the Lord from abroad. The problem was that the Russian Orthodox Church in Russia, as well as in Romania, Bulgaria, and elsewhere in the Slav-accented world, had a most dismal record of total submission to communism. Given its servility, collaboration with the secret police, and undisguised fascist leanings, the official church was hardly in a position to be a moral authority. Also, chasing out other religions smacked of intolerance, and it was a bad start for the new democracies. The very beginning of post-communism had an evangelical stamp on it.

The sports evangelists were already in Cuba. It followed that post-communism was there, too.

I now realized that in addition to Bill and the woman, who had never stopped mouthing the Scriptures the whole time we conversed, there were several other preacherish types with oversized duffel bags, owlish glasses, and proto-pompadours. They were in pretty good physical shape, and I wondered for a moment if these Texas sports preachers were actually some kind of combat unit. A silly thought, I'm sure, but I believe in the creative uses of paranoia. Without it, we wouldn't have any books, movies, or tabloids. But then, of course they were a combat unit. The Pope was going to Cuba, and every Protestant in the free world was probably heading for Cuba to combat the papist empire.

Despite the thrilling presence of the Elvis-pompadoured brigade, I just wasn't getting "that Cuba feeling," the sense that I was going to an enemy country, a dangerous and unpredictable place. Besides the preachers, there were only a few Cubans, looking pretty relaxed, the two Trotsky girls, and some Germans in bright swimming trunks who were definitely going to the beach.

A Cuban couple with tons of luggage—six steamer trunks and what looked like a washing machine in a box—stood by the door, looking out. A mod, *pachuco*-styled dude sprawled against two oversized suitcases with earphones on, flipping through a stack of CDs. The Cuban man by the door noticed me searching about, and came up. He said in Spanish: "My first son is in Washington, the second in Miami. I visited them. Now I'm going home."

I nodded sympathetically. "Must have been difficult leaving Cuba to see them."

He switched to English. "Eh, airplanes go everywhere now. My sons have everything. Washer, drier, microwave. But life is still hard. Home. I go home. My wife cried."

"She wanted to stay in America?"

"Ah, do what? Work to the bones? Better fly home."

"How long do we have to wait?" I asked. "The plane is already two hours late."

He smiled. "I waited a long time; what's two hours?"

After this, our conversation waned, and he went back to stand by his wife's side. I wondered how easy or hard it was for Cubans to visit relatives in the United States. I later found out that if they were in good standing with the Party and were not considered a defection risk, they were allowed a visit every three years.

There really wasn't anyone else to bother. An old farmer type with a straw hat pushed back on his head, and his hands crossed behind his back, turned away his head when I looked at him. He looked sculptural, like something on a stamp, and I wondered if the Cuban secret services placed one such totemic campesino in every port they did business in, to remind foreigners of the dignity, beauty, and classicism of the Cuban peasant through the ages. That would be my kind of secret service. I glanced over at the Trotsky sisters, but they ignored me completely. The Germans gave me the willies. All of the Caribbean, Central America, and South America is crawling with German tourists in bright shorts. Better in shorts than in uniform, of course. Still.

IN THE AIR

How fragile the flesh
        how fragile the world around it
            the life on earth evanescent

—Lawrence Ferlinghetti[22]

The Air Cubana plane was a Russian twin-engine that looked fairly new. We began boarding immediately after it landed, as if, being late, it was now trying to make up with excessive haste. The plane roared off with a dreadful clanking of machinery that sounded as if all the screws and gizmos inside were trying to remember where they belonged. No sooner did we leave the ground than white smoke started filling the cabin. Art looked at me to see if I was worried. I shrugged. I was, even though I had secret information. Jack had told me not to panic if white smoke filled the plane. It was the Russian air-conditioning. Why it blew clouds of smoke was not known. It was something Russian. A German in the seat in front of me stood up waving his arms and screamed, "Mein Gott!"

I tapped him on the shoulder. "I think it's too soon for that!"

He turned around, panicked. "Are you sure?"

"Yes. When the evangelists start praying, that's when you worry, okay? And one more thing. It's not nice to scream and scare everybody."

The captain's slightly hoarse and, I think, rum-soaked voice, hissed and crackled reassuringly over the bad loudspeakers.

"What's he saying?" asked David.

"He's saying that they've elected a new Pope and they are letting out white smoke to let us know."

"This is going to be difficult," David said.

The smoke cleared and I could hear a sigh of relief coursing the length of the aisle. The German collapsed back in his seat and lit a cigarette. On cue, everybody on the plane, including the Trotsky sisters, lit up. The cabin filled with tobacco smoke.

"The world's last all-smoking airline!" said Art, who is allergic to the stuff.

As if sixty cigarette-smoking entities were not enough, lovely

Cuban stewardesses with short dresses and chic short hairdos rolled out carts full of rum and Cohiba cigars. The Cohibas were a wonder to behold. Packed in gorgeous wooden boxes with resplendent wrappers, they were the dream of every cigar lover in the world. A box of twenty-five was $300, which was the going price in Cuba, and a great deal in the U.S. where one Cohiba went for $75 to $100. The Cohiba, Castro's special cigar, was at the center of an international dispute.[23] An American cigar maker, General Cigars, had been marketing a brand called Cohiba, made in the Dominican Republic, with Dominican tobacco. The Cuban export firm Habanos S.A. sued in an international court, alleging, quite sensibly, that General Cigars was trying to pass off phony Cohibas because the real item couldn't be sold legally in the United States. Nobody, claimed Habanos S.A., has been able to duplicate the genuine Cuban seed, or Cuban soil and climate. Indeed, say the smokers. Castro himself, who had been slated for destruction by the CIA with an exploding cigar, was living proof of it. Castro didn't touch the death cigar: it smelled like *Dominican* tobacco.

So when thick cigar smoke mingled with that of cigarettes, the small pressurized cabin took on the consistency of a coal mine on fire. There was nothing to do except to buy a bottle of rum and fire up a Cohiba. Which is what David and I did. Surprisingly, Art did not object terribly to the cigar smoke. The smell had sentimental value. His father had been a cigar smoker, and Art had inherited an extensive collection of cigar cutters. Among connoisseurs, these were highly prized objects. To Art they were mementos of his father and aesthetically pleasing toys.

After we settled down in the clouds, both inside and outside, I looked in "the pocket in front of me" and there found *Granma*, the official organ of the Cuban Communist Party, in Spanish and English editions. With a cozy feeling of sinking into the warm bath of my childhood, I opened the cheaply produced, badly inked Revolutionary organ, and let myself float.

On the front page a smiling, hale-looking Fidel was holding a framed award from the World Health Care conference held in Havana a scant two months before. He had just made a speech "thanking the meeting" for "its statement against the blockade of the island." Fidel's speech, *Granma* informed me, was short by his standards: only four hours. Still, short or not, it was home to a mind-numbing collection of hopeful statistics on the state of Cuban medicine. *Granma* gave readers to understand that Fidel, who had just dropped in to say hi to the delegates, had spoken spontaneously and had remembered these figures without any prepping. This is one of the myths of Fidel: he drops in unexpectedly on a conference, or a marine research vessel, or a gang of surfers, and delivers himself of an amazingly competent speech of three-hour minimum length, containing all pertinent facts and figures. This myth, attested to by wide-eyed witnesses, from newspaper reporters to awed surfers, has helped to give Castro a preternaturally sympathetic aura. Like Stalin, who wrote every book, Castro knows every statistic. The speech to the *health* organization, delivered by a *healthy* Fidel, was excerpted inside *Granma*. It brimmed with *salutary* humor, it contained thunderously *passionate* attacks on imperialism, the embargo, and the United States, and *lively* tributes to Cuba's *health*-care workers. The overwhelming reality of Fidel's health wafted off *Granma* like cigar smoke. Well, I for one, was reassured. I used to read the newspapers of my day, *Scinteia* ("The Spark") and *Scinteia Tinetetului* ("The Spark of Youth"), and remember quite clearly that whenever a dictator was on his deathbed he beamed from the front page with all the retouched glow of a Jerusalem orange. We knew to start celebrating whenever the rosy reports began to report "colds" or "flus." That surely meant that the guy was dead, though it often took the official newspaper and official media about six months to let the rest of us know. Meanwhile, at parades they propped the dead guys on the viewing stand and nobody could tell the difference. Rigor mortis, at least with the Russians, was the favored official pose. I think Brezhnev was reviewing parades dead for three months before anyone noticed.

Next, in order of importance, I read "A Challenge for Women," an article so wooden it could have been written by one of M. Randall's sisters in faith: "Once a greater degree of equality has been attained, as is the general trend on this island, where women constitute the majority of students in higher education, we will be able to aspire to occupying a larger number of leadership positions."

This was worth pondering. Every word was significant. "A greater degree of equality" was nothing less than an admission that Cuban women had a long way to go. And this after years of propaganda about the dizzying heights of equality achieved by Cuban women, thanks to the Revolution. In 1974, "the Cuban woman . . ." according to Margaret Randall, "drives a tractor, hoes a field, and carries an AK-47 as part of her militia duty. She is very likely to do any or all of these with her hair up in curlers, so she will look attractive and feminine to her man at night. The militia and the Army gave her a choice between wearing pants or a skirt."[24]

What an army! Check here, pants or skirt. "Pants line forms to the left, skirts to the right." "Yes, Comrade Sergeant, that will be pants, thank you." "Next!" "Skirt?" All right! Could such a woman, driving a tractor with her hair in curlers, clad in pants, holding an AK-47 and hoeing a field, want anything more? It would seem so. By 1990, "Cuban women were isolated by the very ideology that purported to liberate them. All ideas that did not encourage women to march as commanded by the great patriarch, the *comandante,* were deemed 'diversionary,' enemy propaganda."[25] And then they were marched off to jail, minus the AK-47, the tractor, and the army-issue pants.

The involuntary comedy of communist propaganda was one of the delights of my adolescence. We made a game of isolating some of the most egregious examples, such as the Party Secretary Who Married the Heroic Worker Who'd Had His Balls Eaten by a Pig During Capitalism, and Vera the Small-Arms Seminar Instructor Who Grew Beets with Love. We found all of these characters in the official Stalinist press.

Having been enlightened on the status of the women's struggle, I now turned to "Health in Cuba: An Example of Equity, Solidarity, and Respect," a snappily titled summary of the health conference where a healthy Fidel delivered that most salutary speech. Here I found other statistics. The Cuban health indicators, including their low mortality rate, were similar to those of the United States. And this in the middle of a brutal blockade that was preventing most medicines from reaching Cuba. This *Granma* statistic was true and worthy of respect. The partisans of Cuban socialism always cited the state of Cuban medicine as proof of the goodness of the system. It *was* good, but if there is nothing to eat and the people are dying of hunger, good health care can't do much.

Next, I discovered that "Cuba Modernizes Its Labor Legislation System," an essay that dealt with extremely fine points of Decree-Law 176, concerning labor-management issues and "employment agencies for foreign-investment-based enterprises." This one was hard going even for an old commie-press connoisseur like myself. In Romania we used most of the newspaper to put us to sleep. It was our Valium, especially the great production figures. So many liters of milk, so many cubic tons of corn. These were my lullabies and I slept soundly. In America now I have insomnia: Who can rest after hearing the gruesome crime list on the nightly news? In Romania, the only part of the newspaper that didn't cause somnolence was the sports page. But even there, the scores were subject to Party approval. Anyway, "Cuba Modernizes its Labor Legislation System" had to be read about three or four times before it began to yield the fruit of its meaning. In brief, the "modernization" consisted of the establishment of "work-based labor justice tribunals and the People's Courts." In other words, a new type of repressive institution had been founded to deal with workers. While pondering this, I discovered at the bottom of the page "Van der Veer Sentenced to 15 Years' Imprisonment." Van Der Veer, a freelance lunatic, had been caught running around Havana in fatigues and handing out self-produced raves. He was convicted of "promoting armed activities against Cuba and other acts against state security."

Now, finally, I was starting to get "that Cuba feeling."

I was hoping that after this, *Granma* would let up, and give out some sports scores. It was, after all, only a skimpy couple of folded sheets. But no. In the news flash "Fidel Meets with Cuban Religious Leaders," I found that, in preparation for the Pope's visit, Fidel gathered together the *babalaos*—Santería high priests—and the bishops of the Catholic Church, and amazed them with facts and figures about religion that even they knew nothing of. However, it was not the content of "Fidel Meets with Cuban Religious Leaders" that was significant, but the placement. The article was next to "Raúl Continues Tour Through China." The meaning of this was: Fidel is the good cop, willing to talk to the Pope or to the Devil. Raúl, on the other hand, the intransigent Communist and likely successor of his brother, is talking to the Chinese Communists. After the grievous mistakes that led to the collapse of the Soviet Union, it was clear to the Cubans that the Chinese possessed a better way.

This was not a new opinion. In the early 1960s, Che Guevara was already disgusted by fat Soviet bureaucrats, and admired Mao and the Chinese revolution. The realpolitik of Cuba's relationship with the USSR did not prevent Che from expressing undisguised contempt for the Russians on several occasions. So Raúl was in China, counteracting popery and capitalism. The only trouble was that China didn't give a rat's ass about Cuba. China's relationship with Coca-Cola and AT&T was worth a hundred Cubas. In realistic terms, Cuba should not have mattered much to the USSR, either. If it hadn't been for Khrushchev's ego and the generally quixotic oversensitivities of the cold war, the Cuban Revolution would have remained some sort of African-style socialist experiment evolving slowly into a tourist paradise with a corrupt secret police. Which is not far from what is happening now.

It was time for another swig of rum. *Granma* continued undaunted:

"Sugar Harvest's Priority: Efficiency and Lower Costs." So the sugar wasn't doing too well, either. Well, that was an old story. Finally, *Granma* took pity on me. I read "The Havana Film Festival," an article about the films to be seen, and finally, here were the sports, with a feature on boxer Pablo Lara, '76 Olympian. He was ready for a comeback. There was also a piece about an artist who won a prize, accompanied by a blob of ink that was, I surmised, the prize-winning work.

It was almost over, but for an editorial titled "Lying as a Profession," noting the flood of U.S. lies about Cuba over time, reinforced lately by just-declassified U.S. government documents, dating from 1962 to 1964, which detailed horrific and stupid plans to kill Castro, invade the island, etc. It was not hard to show U.S. stupidity in Cuban affairs: the blunders went back two centuries. Right on.

I put down the paper, exhausted. David handed me back the rum for a swig, without suspecting that I'd just traveled back in time to my childhood.

"Why do they call this paper *Granma*, anyway?" David asked, all innocence like Tom Sawyer.

"It's the name of Castro's boat, the one he landed in to start the Revolution. He bought it in Mexico from an American who'd named it for his grandma and misspelled it. Castro kept the name."

"Pretty cool," David said, "I never got such heavy news from *my* granma."

He had something there. Castro's press was one heavy grandmother.

From the air, the pirate sea—the "Spanish main"—was a sparkling azure mirror. At the bottom were Spanish galleons filled with treasure, airplanes swallowed by the Bermuda Triangle, aircraft sunk by Castro's guns, and tens of thousands of bodies stretching across history, from the conquistadores to the sailors who died on the *Maine*, from pirates to refugees from Castro's paradise. The Caribbean was the grim repository of a violent history.

"Caked with corsairs" is how a writer in 1934 described the sixteenth-century water.[26] I looked down, trying to see ghosts.

On October 27, 1492, Columbus sailed from Santo Domingo and found a paradise of palm trees, exotic flowers, hummingbirds that were "like animated particles of the rainbow," and also the peace-loving Taino, who lived without guile, in communal harmony. The landscape brought rhapsodic cries from his quill: "It is the most beautiful land human eyes have ever beheld, full of good harbors and profound rivers." As for the natives, Columbus entered in his journal his intention "to free the friendly, simple people and convert them to the holy faith." This was, unfotunately, an impulse that has proved irresistible to almost every foreigner since. The communistic Taino served utopists like Jean-Jacques Rousseau as models for their "noble savage," and ended up in the very foundation of Marx and Engels's theory of communism. The Taino, who were promptly wiped out by the Spaniards and by the fiercer native Caribs, who resented the Taino's welcome to the Spaniards, never knew that they would also be responsible for the distant utopia of Fidel Castro. Thus all things come around to taste their own tails. Columbus, of course, thought that he had, at long last, found India or China, the land of the Khan, spices, gold, silk. And died before he was proved wrong by Sebastián de Ocampo, who circumnavigated Cuba in 1508 and found it to be an island.

Christopher Columbus was going to be buried in Cuba. His remains were brought from Santo Domingo in 1796 and placed in the cathedral in Havana. He rested there for about a century and was slated to be the centerpiece of the very grand Cristóbal Colón Cemetery being built in Havana in the nineteenth century. But when Cuba won its independence from Spain, the Spaniards whisked him back and buried him in Seville, thus making Columbus Cuba's first political exile. It would have been better if he hadn't found the island at all. Cuba quickly became the gateway for the conquest of the Americas. It was here that Hernán Cortés resupplied his conquistadores for the assault against the Aztec empire. Bernal Díaz, in his soldier's account of the conquest, describes thus the provisioning of Mexico-bound ships in Cuba: "We found ourselves in possession of three ships loaded with cassava bread, which is made from a root, and we bought pigs, which cost us three pesos each. At the time there were no sheep or cattle in the island of Cuba, for it was only beginning to be settled."[27]

In 1997, as I was to find out, that was pretty much still the economy of Cuba, except that pigs were a little more expensive. There still seemed to be little beef for sale on the island of Cuba, 481 years after Bernal Díaz wrote those lines. All cows are now the sacred property of the state: stealing one is punishable by ten years in prison.

"Fee, fi, fo, fum!" David passed the rum. There was plenty of gold at the bottom of the sea. The city of Havana rose below us in hues of yellow and brown, like a basket of bananas and melons, the nose of the El Morro fortress pointing into the azure water.

HAVANA

In the summer of 1960 I went to Havana. On July 26 Fidel Castro would always deliver a mammoth speech in Revolutionary Square and he needed people to fill the square. Over a thousand of us young men were packed into a sugarcane train and we arrived in Havana after a trip of almost three days. Most of us were sexually aroused on that train; all those sweaty bodies pressing together.

—Reinaldo Arenas, *Before Night Falls*[28]

The smell of Havana seemed familiar. As we crowded into the small Lada taxi, I breathed in Latin America: fried food, diesel, humidity, ocean salt. This was the gasoline tropic. The road from the airport was crowded with smoke-spewing trucks, old American cars, motorcycles with sidecars, mule-drawn carts, and thousands of sturdy, Chinese-made bicycles. These bicycles, known as "flying pigeons," made the road look like postwar Rome in a Vittorio De Sica film. There were also streams of pedestrians, thin men in loose pants and threadbare shirts who looked as if they'd been walking since the dawn of time. The women walking alongside the men were equally thin, though the young ones wore miniskirts and plastic sandals. The sidecars of the motorcycles were full of children. Many girls were riding on the handlebars of bicycles pedaled by shirtless young men. The highway was dotted with huge faded billboards of Che Guevara with slogans: "Patria o Muerte," "Socialismo o Muerte," "Hasta la Victoria Siempre." Buildings from every historical period were peeling in a jumble of sun-washed colors. We were driving through time in a crazy loop-de-loop.

We were headed for Vedado, a once-stylish quarter of Havana where the villas of the oligarchs mingled with the pleasure palaces of American gangsters. Water-streaked socialist building blocks rose in the distance. Meyer Lansky and Leonid Brezhnev decayed together above an earlier, more understated elegance.

Every man, from taxi driver to porter to briefcase-toting bureaucrat, was dark, husky, and hirsute. I was back in the world of men with mustaches. The mustache, the risen parenthesis, the sickle moon of Latin as well as Mediterranean machismo, is the signature of a world where emotions still rule, where the laws are still subordinate to men, where efficiency has not yet clean-shaved darkness, moisture, and mystery from the world. "A kiss without a mustache is like an egg without salt," say the Romanians. The mustache, depressing like Nietzsche's, fierce like Kublai Khan's, extravagant like Dalí's, or impotent like Hitler's, is the single most important bio-orthographic symbol of the sad, garbled text of humanity. Cuban men were men of bushy mustaches, not quite as wild as those of Pancho Villa's Mexicans, but fiercely expressive all the same. This being said, I must now add that Cuban mustaches grew mostly on men over thirty-five, many of whom have some kind of official legitimacy, if not actually a police function. I soon observed that young people, as well as Western-styled apparatchiks, were clean-shaven in pointed defiance of the regime. Fidel Castro and Che Guevara's extreme hairiness, seen in the context of the sixties, was quite heroic. All those beards, mustaches, and heads of hair were flung like whips at the establishment of bankers with barbers and bourgeois men with nothing better to do than to abdicate their manhood each morning before the mirror. Long hair, a good beard, a fierce mustache—those were weapons! In light of the revolutionary nature of follicles it is more than ironic that in the late 1960s and 1970s, Fidel's policemen descended like steel dragonflies on Cuba's artistic, longhaired youth, and shaved their heads bare. The hairy Revolutionaries became hairy tyrants.

The longhairs, an official commentator declared in 1968, organized in "bands of schizophrenics" with names like "Los Beats" or "Los Chicos Melenudos" (Longhaired Boys); they "hung about listening to imperialist jukeboxes" and "danced madly to epileptic music." The result was "mass shavings of long-haired men and the departure of mini-skirted girls, who were said to have made 'passionate love in their school-uniforms,' to forced labor camps in the countryside."[29]

In 1997, only the mustache remained, a vanishing reminder of the hair wars of the 1960s. Resistance to the regime was confined to T-shirts with American corporate logos on them, or, for the more daring, unabashedly defiant tattoos.

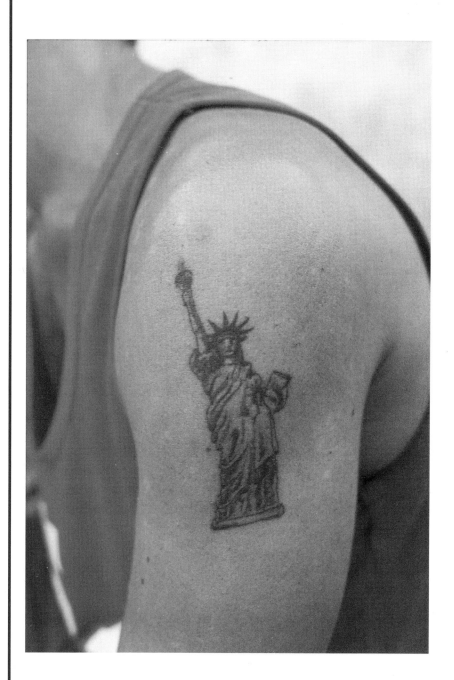

Miss Liberty, defiant

DAY ONE: "UNDERAGE FUSION BROUGHT ME THIS FAR"

exquisite corpse no. 1

Underage fusion brought me this far
When the Pope kisses Castro a plume of black smoke will spew & they will
    both croak
And the Lord said: let the bubbles rise to a veritable throb.
Communist lava congealed with Buicks
hitchhike on the Popemobile.
The corpses of generals are full of sugar.
Will there be a crystal through which to see the world?
Pig skin, pork snouts, ways out.

—**Ariel Pena, David Graham, Art Silverman, and Andrei Codrescu (while
eating indifferent fish at Capri Hotel restaurant)**

EXPLICATION

The above poem is an "exquisite corpse." In order to write an exquisite corpse, the participants pass around a sheet of paper. Each person writes a line of verse and folds the paper over it, leaving a single word visible. The next person will then write another line, using the word left showing, then fold the paper, leaving a word visible to inspire the next person, and so on. Any number can participate. When the sheet is all written, the person who wrote the last line will unfold it and read it out loud to everyone, thus revealing with X-ray precision the collective mind of the participants. This form of poetry was invented by French surrealist poets in the 1920s and has been practiced by poets whenever they are together in clandestine and seductive situations.

Art Silverman suggested that we write a corpse in every new place we visit in Cuba, if possible. It was a brilliant suggestion. During the ten days that we were on the island we produced nineteen exquisite corpses, which taken together constitute a rich, collective poetic, sensual, and physical description of our adventures, as well as a record of

Cuban realities. The authors were, for the most part, Art, David, myself, and the fourth member of our crew, Ariel Pena. We were joined, on occasion, by others.

The reader of poetry could easily reconstruct our journey from these corpses, which will head every section of the story that follows. In deference to those who find poetry difficult, I will also provide a narrative, which, unlike the poems, will emphasize mainly my own heroic role in the events, because, naturally, I am the solo author of the narrative. Given this predisposition toward megalomania (common to all solo authors), I advise the reader to check carefully with the accompanying corpse. Wherever I seem to be overly cozy with myself, the corpse will provide a corrective, and if there is any contradiction, I suggest that the reader take the corpse's account as the more accurate of the two. I suggest also that the reader not take lightly the metaphor of the exquisite corpse, which is meant to represent Cuba. Yes, Cuba is an exquisite corpse (though a very sexy one).

I will now introduce the reader to the Capri Hotel and to our amazing fourth musketeer, Ariel Pena. I will also explain the references in "Exquisite Corpse No. 1," while providing, at the same time, a suspenseful narration of the events.

The caged parakeets were screeching very loudly in the huge lobby of the Capri Hotel, formerly Meyer Lansky's casino. The gaming tables had been replaced by a few ratty couches, now occupied by visitors with film fest badges, mostly Latin American men with trim mustaches, in blue jeans, and their female counterparts in short skirts, with well-manicured toes protruding from fashionable sandals. Around their necks hung the Film Fest badges, all-important identification that gave its wearers first seating privileges at the new films being shown and allowed them, as well, to walk unmolested into tourist hotels.

A number of more lushly mustachioed guys in guayabera shirts, with bulging walkie-talkies, leaned against the reception desk and clustered around a small table to the right of the entrance. At the small rum-and-coffee bar at the far end of the lobby, a sleepy waitress was watching a Brazilian soap opera on TV.

I didn't see it at first because, to me, it looked familiar: a ten-foot Christmas tree twinkled to the right of the entrance. What drew my attention to it was the people on the other side of the plate-glass window, looking at it. They stood on the sidewalk, pressed against the glass, staring in as if they had just sighted a movie star. At first I thought that this was what was going on, and I looked around to see if some fabulously famous person was in the lobby. But the only star was the one at the top of the Christmas tree. It was decorated with what looked like antique colored bulbs, dolls, and paper birds.

One of the security guys saw me looking. "The first Christmas tree in Cuba," he said neutrally.

"For the Pope?" I asked.

"For Catholics."

Checking in was as easy as getting a driver's license in New Orleans, which is to say slow. But once in possession of our "Tarjetas de Huésped" (Guest Cards), which we were advised never to part with, we were free to occupy our rooms. I believe that the entire process of admission was conducted manually by the desk clerk, though two computers rose proudly from the counter. A flower pot sat on top of one of them, while the other was lovingly covered with a crocheted cloth. I had observed the quaint custom of decorating a (mostly nonfunctioning) computer with pretty objects at a Mexican travel office a couple of years before. It was a Latin thing.

My sixth-floor room was well used. The ratty shag carpet was the texture of ground cigarette ash, and the bed sagged to its last springs under a thin, weathered mattress. The sheets and pillows had the rough feel of ten thousand launderings. One of the bedside lamps worked, throwing a yellow circle of tungsten brightness on the bed. The other was dead. A partition divided me from the room next door. The window gave onto a vista of the much larger National Hotel, where most of the film festival delegates were housed. A number of Brezhnev-vintage apartment buildings loomed beyond. The street below was rife with humanity. Every corner had a few idle boys and girls leaning casually against walls and lampposts, smoking cigarettes and looking up at the hotel windows now and then. It was seven p.m. in Havana, Cuba. The afternoon sky was milky blue, brushed with wisps of cloud over the sea. I smelled the brine in the breeze.

I dropped my bags on the bed, filled my pockets with the bounty of Wal-Mart, and descended the 1950s elevator to meet Art and David in the lobby. The room and the elevator put me in an indescribably happy mood, caused doubtless by the similarity, down to the tiniest smell, between the Capri and the Bucharest hotel by the same name where I'd stayed in 1965, before leaving Romania. Say what you might about socioeconomic-political-religious conditions, the fact remains that all places in all times can be known and connected by smell. There is a commie smell as sure as there is a fascist smell. The commie smell was here, transporting me right back in time. I was suddenly nineteen years old, defiant, irreverent, filled with an insatiable appetite for the unknown.

There was no way I could explain this to my companions who were waiting for me in the lobby, looking fairly excited but also cautious.

"It's my world," I exclaimed. "The police are watching! Love is in the air!"

They looked me over. Would there be psychological difficulties?

Capri birds

We were waiting for our translator, Ariel Pena. Art had contacted her from Washington. Ariel was married to the BBC correspondent in Havana, Tom Gibb, and was coming highly recommended as someone knowledgeable in all things Cuban. I was not sure whether we needed a translator or not, but I didn't feel confident enough in my rudimentary Spanish to take on the job. Art had some Spanish, and David had zip.

I was impatient to take on the streets whose tropical pull I could feel, and I was starving. I was also looking forward to Ariel's arrival, because I get very impatient in the company of men. I think of hell as a place where there are only men. The army and jail are perfect examples of it.

ARIEL PENA

I said it in Hebrew—I said it in Dutch—
I said it in German and Greek;
But I wholly forgot (and it vexes me much)
That English is what you speak!

—Lewis Carroll, *The Hunting of the Snark*[30]

It was immediately apparent that the petite brunette with the deep black Mayan eyes and faded blue jeans was no mere translator. There was an elegant restraint in her manner, and an insistent thoughtfulness. She spoke an exquisite, educated Spanish and a British-Spanish-accented soigné English. I liked her instantly, as did my companions. Indeed, Ariel turned out to be a meta-translator, who did not carry meanings back and forth merely between languages but also between cultures. She translated Cuba as much as the Cubans' words. Over the next ten days, I pieced together her story, which was extraordinary. A ex-FMLN (Faribundo Martí Liberation Front) guerrilla fighter from El Salvador, she had had an adventurous and unpredictable life. Her evolution from communist revolutionary to tough-minded analyst of Cuban realities was astounding. She provided us with the details of a world she had gotten to know for profound personal reasons.

Ariel looked at the Christmas tree. "I have never seen one in Cuba. Last year at the tobacco factory near the Capitol, the workers received permission to put up a Christmas tree. They made ornaments in their spare time, and some of them brought ornaments out of dusty attics where they'd been hiding them. At last, the tree shined, but on Christmas Day, which is not a holiday here, the *ideológico* came and pulled the tree down, ornaments crashing to the floor. He called a factory-wide meeting and raved for hours about 'counterrevolutionary attitudes,' 'sabotage,' and 'socialist Cuba.'"

The permission, it seems, had come prematurely, from someone who lost his job afterward. There had been some kind of struggle within the Communist Party, and someone had jumped the gun. Fidel Castro had dropped the ban on believers in 1991, but no Catholic could be a member of the Party. The premature Christmas tree must have sneaked in between policies.

"This happens a lot," Ariel said. "Somebody high up gives an order, then someone countermands it. Even Castro changes his mind. What are the people to understand? Nobody knows what is allowed and what isn't, or why and when. That's how you drive a child insane, how you infantilize people and drive them crazy."

Ariel had thought about these things. Once she had been a fanatical *ideológico* herself. Now there appeared a sadness in her voice, and a sense of shame and contrition. But then she brightened up and said: "Do you know why the Pope is coming to Cuba? To visit hell, to meet the Devil, and to see why eleven milion people still believe in miracles."

It was our first Cuban joke.

We settled for the hotel restaurant for dinner because we were too hungry to eat elsewhere. We had our first Cuban meal: indifferent fish fried in cornmeal, *congris* (black beans and rice together shaped in a little tower), french fries, and papaya. (The alternative to fish was a pork dish of snouts and skins.) And we wrote the above corpse, in whose body certain constant motifs of our Cuban trip were already present. The image of the Pope kissing Castro came from our discussion of what was going to happen during the Pontiff's visit. My opinion was that something big was doubtless going to happen, because whenever huge crowds gathered, the potential for revolution was very great. I based this opinion on the Romanian revolt of 1989, when mobs had begun spontaneously singing forbidden songs and shouting improvised slogans against the tyranny. Cubans were highly musical people. But Ariel cooled down such imaginings by pointing out that the Cuban people were too dispirited for revolt. They were literally starving. Most of the dissidents were in exile. Castro's support among the poorest of the poor was still, amazingly, holding, in a mystical and unreal form. Besides, the Pope was hardly an incendiary presence. He would command mostly baffled respect.

In this, as in many other things, Ariel was right. Still, if revolt wasn't in the cards, there was still the surreal moment of the "kiss," when the two exhausted old men might collapse in each other's arms and die. This might have come to pass, but the two men didn't kiss. They merely shook hands. In Cuba the Pope didn't even kiss the ground, as he usually did, but kissed instead a box of dirt that was raised up to him. His creaky joints weren't up to sprawling on the tarmac any longer.

"Communist lava congealed with Buicks" was the result of our having observed an inordinate number of old American cars on the way in from the airport. All these 1950s automobiles, the newest dating from the fateful year 1959, had been left behind by exiles and were now being cared for with extraordinary craft by their new owners, who had turned most of them into taxis.

We discussed the history of Cuba, its endless wars and revolutions, its generals and dictatorships. It was a bitter history, unfolding, ironically, against a background of sugar, the island's main product. The "corpses of generals" were indeed full of sugar, but they were hardly sweet. The Capri Hotel restaurant, we later found out, had been a favorite meeting place for dissidents in the late 1960s. They came here to drink coffee and plot some improbable exit from Cuban history through sex, rock 'n' roll, and poetry. The best some of them did was to plot an exit from the island, but history was harder to shake; it followed like a rabid dog.

"And the Lord said: let the bubbles rise to a veritable throb," was a line that one of us macho guys had penned in obscure response to Ariel's undoubtedly heady presence.

We had throbbing hot, thick, sweet Cuban coffee. We were ready to hit the streets. Our crew was complete. Our imaginations were stimulated.

HAVANA STREETS

The *jineteros* and *jineteras* jammed in front of the hotel entrance swarmed around us like a happy flock of hummingbirds. *Jinetero* is Cuban for "hustler," and it can mean anything from prostitute to self-appointed tour guide or penniless dance lover. The women were bare-legged, dressed in short skirts or body-hugging Lycra, and spanned the color spectrum from Mediterranean white to lustrous ebony. The sounds of salsa from the disco next door had them on the move, hips wiggling, torsos shimmying, hands playing invisible maracas. The boys gave off the same signals, though they were not as overtly sexual as the girls, and offered themselves as tour guides. The girls offered, well, everything.

Most of them were young, barely sixteen, but they were unmistakably women, self-possessed and most aware of the effect their surging bodies had on men. There were no *jineteras* over eighteen. After that age they must have married and led normal lives. Hustling was some kind of initiation. David said: "Where do they keep the older women?"

The Gang: David, Art,
Ariel, and moi (left to
right)

"There aren't any," Art said. "It's a country of young girls."

Ariel's presence deterred them only briefly, though the girls did approach her first, asking where she was from and trying to ascertain what her relationship to us was. This was their way of asking permission to capture us. It was an open and friendly exchange. Ariel explained that it would never occur to any Cuban woman to deny a *jinetera's* right to a tourist, unless she was married to the man. The assumption that all foreigners were there to help Cubans from starving was deeply held. Ariel, honest to a fault, answered the *jineteras'* questions earnestly. She treated them with dignity and interest, without a trace of condescension, an attitude for which they were grateful. In fact, nearly every stranger who came into contact with us for whatever reason conceived instant respect and sympathy for Ariel, whose entire being seemed to communicate an unassuming simplicity. Ariel made no big deal of her position with us—she was, after all, a translator, someone who made good money—and generally let us fend for ourselves in situations involving the locals, figuring (not always rightly) that we were big boys who could take care of ourselves.

Two of the beauties with the most insistent eyes draped themselves like clusters of grapes on my arms and fired off questions in snippets of Italian, German, Russian, and English. When they discovered that we were from the United States their enthusiasm became boundless. My left side said: "My aunt and my cousins are in Miami. You know them? Beautiful girls! You go dance with them, okay?" My right rejoined: "My father is in Detroit. I hate him." They were not making this up. Everything about them, including their intentions, was transparent. They were candid and fearless.

"You don't believe me," said my right. "Why would I lie to you? All I want is for you to take me dance. Maybe we drink a Coca."

Ariel confirmed that most of these girls were not prostitutes. Many of them were college girls or young professionals out for a night on the town. There were even some doctors among the *jineteras*. At Cuban salaries of ten to fifteen dollars a month, none of them could afford the discos' entrance fees. They were not averse to having a meal bought for them, and for a small present, they would gladly go to bed with their date. Cuban girls, Ariel said, were sexually experienced from a very young age.

Art and David were doing their best to fend off other teenagers who undulated about them in their platform sandals, making multilingual siren sounds.

"I am religious," David protested. "I only love the Virgin." The schoolgirl in her polka-dot blouse and miniskirt who leaned against him like a steady sweetheart assumed an angelic expression and, placing her hand loosely on her thigh, exclaimed, "I am a virgin. Can't you tell?"

The half block between the Capri and the National Hotels in Havana was awash in adolescent concupiscence and cheap perfume. We negotiated it with the utmost difficulty and were abandoned with regret only at the entrance to the National, where the *jineteras* were forbidden to enter. A tourist confined to this area would get an image of joyous, sensual Afro-Cubans, an image as clichéd as "happy pickaninnies." The irony, if that's what it was, was that the Revolution had professed to free Cuban blacks from just such clichés.

The National was both grander and more conspicuously policed than the Capri. We had to show our *tarjetas* and explain to a distinctly hostile civilian that Ariel was our translator. He directed us to get film festival badges as soon as possible, and waved us in.

The grandeur that was once Lucky Luciano's embraced us with its columns, fanciful lighting, grand stairway, wall frescoes, and terraces. Music wafted from discreetly placed ensembles near bars hidden in tropical foliage and blooms. The scents of bougainvillea and jasmine mingled with the perfume on the necks and arms of evening-gowned beauties with jet-black hair, dancing in the arms of dashing young film stars. The opening party of the film festival was in full swing. Miraculously, we found seats on a rattan couch before a low table and lowered ourselves into the pure fantasy of an exotic night that gave no hint of being shared with the groaning masses of socialist Cuba. That is, it would have given no hint if I had not begun listening to the song which the black-clad singer of the band by the bar belted out with all the passion of his Afro-Cuban heart: "Your beloved presence, Che Guevara, Comandante Che Guevara, Querido Comandante . . ." It was the Che Guevara song, a romantic tribute to the Revolutionary hero, a song whose melody began to haunt us all through our stay in Cuba until one night, at the Hotel Grande in Santiago de Cuba, I made a desperate bet that we would hear it twelve more times before we left the island in two days. David bet six times. Ariel, five. Art, two. I won. But that evening, the song sounded profoundly beautiful. The two impeccably dressed couples at the table next to ours applauded wildly and, while tipping the band, requested them to play another Communist Top-Ten hit, "Mañana Compañeros."

Art rose to tip the band, too, and discovered that they were selling a tape that included the Che Guevara song. "How many pesos?" he asked. "Pesos?" replied the indignant singer. "Ten dollars. Dollars."

"There is something here Che wouldn't be too happy about," Art said when he came back.

David bought a fat cigar, and we ordered, at Ariel's suggestion, Planter's Punch, which our waitress pronounced "Poonch." It was a lemonady concoction of dark rum, lemons, and a sprig of mint, that produced an instant beneficial surge.

At this point, Ariel made her exit, pleased, I think, with our gang. Not long after, Art did the same, claiming that one Poonch was enough to rob him of reason. Knowing him as I did, I knew that he had been practically wild. This was the longest time I ever remember Art enjoying the mindless pleasure of a drink, without taping the sounds of the ice cubes or something.

David and I stayed on, valiant knights, and ordered more Poonch.

I had just become absorbed by the sinuous grace of a Hispanic beauty who wore a white flower in her hair and was dancing with a midget producer, when I felt the merest touch on my shoulder, the feathery brush of an angel's wing.

"Do you have a light?" sang a husky but girlish voice. I looked up into a mess of curly black hair.

"Can we sit here with you?" Julie asked, and before I could say anything, Julie and Ysemina floated onto the rattan opposite from us and trained the reflectors of their eyes on the two Yankees.

"He looks like John Travolta," Ysemina told Julie.

Julie studied David for a long second. "Definitely," she said.

I translated this for David, who looked impassive, and then I asked, "Who do I look like?"

Julie picked up my empty Poonch glass and stared intently at the ice cubes and the sprig of mint stuck there. "Sting," she said.

I leave this to my readers to judge.

"Do you read ice cubes and mint?"

"Like a hand," said Julie. "Cubans read everything. Tea, coffee, hands, cracks . . ."

"Cracks?"

"Yes. Cracks in the street, in the walls, in the ceiling. In Cuba everything is cracked." She started laughing helplessly, like a schoolgirl. Ysemina cracked up, too.

"What are they laughing about?" asked David.

"You," I said. "They think you're cracked."

"Why do Cubans read everything?"

Julie leaned over, nearly touching my face, and whispered. "To find out about the future. See when the Crazy One dies, nobody knows what will happen. Do you want me to read your hand?"

That was pretty daring of Julie, but as I would find out in the coming days, waiting for "the Crazy One" to die was a common Cuban pastime.

"Sure, go ahead." Julie took my hand and looked carefully at the paths carved there by the Fates. "A lot of girls," she said. "One of them is me. Wait, I'll write over these other girls. Do you have a pen?"

I gave her my felt-tip pen. She wrote her name, address, and telephone number on my palm.

Tropical breeze, beautiful girls, flowers, the smell of the sea, big stars above, the proximity of the equator, black, liquid woman's eyes . . . Another Planter's Poonch would have put me under the spell of romance. I was aware that all harbors are hypnotic, like the insides of flowers, and that Havana was the first harbor of the New World. With some difficulty, and only after promising to call next day, we took our leave of the two young women.

"How do you suppose they got into the hotel?" asked David, as we shook our heads no to the seductive entreaties of the girls on the street.

I suspected that Cuba, like Romania, was in that stage of its development when everything could be had for one dollar.

THE POWER OF PRAYER

I looked at my watch before I took it off. It was two a.m., the bed was lumpy, and I felt charged with energy. I wrote in my notebook, trying to capture in words Julie's vanilla scent, the silky air, the paunch of the fat man mouthing the Che song, the cigar smoke. A sickle moon was plastered against the window. When I finally lay down, I drifted off immediately. Not for long. From behind the partition separating my room from the one next to it, came a deep man's voice, charged with dramatic emotion:

"THANK YOU, LORD! THANK YOU, LORD, FOR YOUR SPECIAL CREATION, FOR THIS BLESSED PEOPLE AND

THEIR MUSIC! YOU FILL ME WITH JOY AND ETERNAL PLEASURE!"

This powerful appeal to the Lord was followed by a weak woman's voice, whispering in accented English: "Thank you, Lord!"

"LOUDER, DAUGHTER! LOUDER! HE CAN'T HEAR YOU IF YOU WHISPER! THANK YOU, LORD! GRACIAS, SEÑOR! I SEE THE LIGHT! THANK YOU, LORD!"

I stood bolt upright in my bed, not sure if I'd died and gone to Texas. The man's accent was definitely Texan, and it belonged in a country church. We were in Cuba, for Chrissakes! What the hell was going on?

I banged on the partition. "Excuse me, good Christians, but what do you think you're doing yelling in the middle of the night!"

"Pardon us sinners!" came the preacher's booming voice, addressed to, I'm not sure, either me or the Lord. "I've been bringing another soul to the Lord!"

"Fine," I said, "Just do it quietly."

The racket ceased and I lay back down on the bed. Soon there was some fervent whispering, and then some rustling and heavy motion like a body being pummelled, and I heard the girl weep. I stood bolt upright. Had the preacher murdered the girl? I picked up the phone to call the front desk, but then I remembered: I was in Cuba. Besides, there was no dial tone. I had to take care of business myself. There was some walking back and forth behind the partition, then some whispering, then what sounded like the counting of money. By this time, I'd dressed quietly and was holding my camera like a rock, fully prepared to slam the Texas fellow and liberate the crying woman. I heard the door swing open next door, and close.

Presumably alone, the preacher lapsed heavily onto his soggy bed whose springs creaked, and sighed with what I could have sworn was a drunken slur, "Blessed be the meek. . . ."

Next morning, I rose from a troubled sleep, put on a clean shirt, and, without bothering to shave, went out. Just outside my door, wafting on a cloud of Old Spice, was my old acqauintance and next-room neighbor, Bill Huxley, sports evangelist. He looked hearty, hale, and freshly shaven, and he had a music case on his back.

"Reverend Huxley," I said, "was that a sports star in your room last night?"

He laughed uproariously. "Why, not at all, that was a *jinetera*!"

I must have looked angry, because he hastened to explain. He told me that in addition to sports evangelism, which was pretty slim pickings, his mandate also called for driving hustlers away from sin and to the Lord. What he did was pay the girls the money they'd have gotten by spending the night in sin, and then preach to them about Christ instead, by using examples drawn from his own life, particularly the joys of fidelity and marriage.

Recalling all the odd noises of his sermonizing, I asked him what that was about. "Sounded more like a beating than praying, to be quite honest, Rev."

"At the end, when they accept Christ, I lay hands on them and we pray together. We pray out loud, and the girls sometimes cry and let loose some awful spirits. Sometimes I break down myself, but because you demanded your sleep, we prayed quietly."

Well, if that was quiet, I hated to think what loud was. I thanked him nonetheless for his consideration, but the vision of this beefy, gray-pompadoured fellow laying his big, sweaty hands on the bare chocolate shoulders of a poor *jinetera* like Julie gave me the creeps. In their place, I'd much rather perform the furtive but thankfully brief motions of paid sex.

I asked Reverend Huxley what the instrument on his back was for.

"I play the trumpet," he said, "on the street, at the train station, at the airport. Folks come and join me in song. Sometimes they bring their own instruments. I then lay down the trumpet and tell them what I know about the things that changed my life."

Playing music on the street had been forbidden until the late 1980s. Then the Soviets kicked the bucket, and the musicians took over. Geraldo Piloto, the composer for the salsa band Klimax, said, "Cubans live on music the way others live on bread and water."[31] That was the literal truth.

We rode the elevator down in silence. At the bottom, Huxley was joined by a white-haired fellow I'd never seen, and two of the other sports evangelists from the plane. They were all carrying music cases. It was soul-collecting time at the train station in Havana. Blow that trumpet, Gabriel!

But if Yankee religious trumpeting was safe, some Cuban music was not. The popular group Charanga Habanera had been banned for playing for six months for singing "Hey green mango, now that you're ripe, why haven't you fallen yet?"[32] Everyone knows that for the past thirty-five years the big mango in Cuba has worn green fatigues.

I met Art and David for breakfast at the hotel restaurant and told them about my night. Our sojourn was beginning in proper surrealist order. The breakfast buffet was surprisingly good: papaya, grapefruit juice, eggs, fresh rolls, sausage, and—one mango. This was no communist repast. The mango was ripe.

DAY TWO: "TWITCH: SO LITTLE OR TOO LONG, *AMIGO*"

exquisite corpse no. 2

Twitch: so little or too long, *amigo*
Mojito Mass, Il Papa
will have a rice and mango day—
Al Lewis' least favorite Pope
is the current one.
Love and kisses and all that shit!
With teeth!
City lights, foul harbor, chains of gold
the cocoon is open, exposed—
At the National Adrenaline Hotel Cuba
the laughs go on *every momentito!*

—**Art Silverman, David Graham, Ariel Pena, Andrei Codrescu, and Al Lewis**

AL LEWIS

Yes, Al Lewis. In the lobby, the hotel parakeets were making a huge racket right above the world-famous head of Grandpa on *The Munsters.* Sprawled on a couch, smoking an extra-long cigar, was the eighty-seven-year-old Lewis, energetically holding forth to a group of Venezuelans, whose idol he clearly was. Al's booming voice was telling the Venezuelans and whoever else might have been listening that Cuba would never revert to being an American–United Fruit Company–Mafia colony again, no matter what happened to Fidel Castro, who was pretty young anyway, and going to live to one hundred, thank you. He himself, Al Lewis, eighty-seven years old, had been chain-smoking cigars for forty-five years, and had no plans to either die or give them up.

Al Lewis, it turns out, had been coming to Cuba since the early fifties to frolic with gamblers and actors. He'd hung out in Meyer Lansky's entourage with tough characters like the actor George Raft.

"At the time," Al told us, "Havana used to be the most glamorous whorehouse. Americans used to come in droves."

After the Revolution, with which he sympathized, he kept on coming to Cuba. "Some of the personalities of the Revolution I met. Malcolm X. Che Guevara." And then, for our benefit: "There are no stupider people on earth than the Americans. They don't know history. You have more colors than Benetton here."

Al laughed his raucous signature laugh, setting off all his listeners. This was the laugh that could be heard on cable around the world.

I asked him how Cuba had changed since the Russians left.

"You have to understand. Like people, countries have an agenda. I'm not interested in the Soviets' agenda. Maybe they wanted a bumblebee in the backyard of the United States. In a way, Cubans prospered with the Soviets. It was also negative for the Cubans, they put all their fruit in one basket. But then comes this—what? Blockade or embargo?—I would challenge you to go all through Havana and find a bottle of aspirin. Example. My wife had a headache. The doctor couldn't look in her ear with his thingamajig because he had no battery. Had to tilt her head to the light in the window. Whenever I come here, my wife and I bring a giant suitcase full of medicine. Last year we met a friend, a doctor. I brought him those small IV needles. He started to cry. He had not seen them in three years. To me, I'm not interested in labels, communist, socialist, whatever. To me, that's criminal. Obscene. That doctor did not have those little needles. For children. So things have changed. Going through a bad time now. I'm a human being who has lived and observed for eighty-seven years. I've seen the repairs they've done. They have the best health system, the best literacy rate."

Satisfied, but not exhausted, Al leaned back and took a tremendous puff from his cigar. Castro was lucky. Al was the best English-speaking friend he had. That laughter alone was pure gold. And he was convincing. The embargo was indeed a tragedy for the Cuban people, especially for the most vulnerable among them, children and the very poor. The Communist Party apparatchiks got along, as did those lucky enough to have relatives in the United States who sent them dollars. The rest, the majority of Cubans, had neither food nor medicine. That was the work of the embargo, which was the work of right-wing exiles and conservative cold warriors.

"What's the secret of your youth?" I asked Al, handing him the "exquisite corpse" sheet, on which he scribbled a line without flinching.

"'How old would you be if you didn't know how old you was?' My secret is all I do. I don't like old people. I chase young girls. *Chase* them. Don't catch them. If I catch them, that will make me old. Someone asked George Burns how sex was at his age, and George said, 'It's like playing pool with a rope.' Wouldn't want that."

All the women listening gasped with delight. He was a charming old fox, Al Lewis, who'd been in more movies than he could remember. I bought him a Zombie, his drink of choice: three kinds of rum, plus grenadine. "I drink them all day," he said. For the throngs of his Havana fans who sought him out like the Sphinx in the lobby of the Capri, he was Grandpa. "Wherever there is electricity," Al said, "there I am." His line had been: "With love and kisses and all that shit! With teeth!"

Six months later, in May 1998, the eighty-eight-year-old Al Lewis announced that he would run for governor of New York on the Green Party ticket against the incumbent Republican, George Pataki.

THE GOAT

Later that morning, Ariel arrived with exciting news. We were going to a Santería ceremony. I had thought that Santería, along with Catholicism, had long been banished from the kingdom of socialism.

Al Lewis

On the contrary, Ariel explained, Santería is now encouraged by the state in Cuba. The *babalaos* are invited in costume to all the state functions, visible symbols of the oft-invoked Afro-Cuba. Although most high-ranking Party officials are white, of Galician extraction, like Castro, there is a great deal of lip service being paid to Afro-Cuban culture. July 26, the anniversary of Fidel's abortive attack on the Moncada military barracks in the 1950s, is the official Cuban holiday, and until this year, it stood for Christmas and every other holy day. The *babalaos* blessed July 26 because they believed that Fidel was the Chosen One, a saint. As proof of his sainthood, they cited a Cuban film in which a white dove sits on El Líder's shoulder as he addresses the masses on January 1, 1959. He was pictured with the dove in cheap lithographs for popular consumption for a number of years—until his images were officially withdrawn from circulation, this to better enforce the myth of his ubiquity and omnipotence. Like God, he became both ubiquitous and invisible. Fidel was also a magus, said the *babalaos*, because he went to Nigeria and learned a secret spell by means of which he killed his chief rival, the Miami-based Cuban leader Jorge Mas Canosa. Mas Canosa, the Máximo of the Miami right-wingers, had dropped dead of a rather mysterious heart attack in November 1997. The *babalaos* also pointed to the sign language of El Máximo's hands during his speeches—"beats *listening* to them," said Ariel—which, they said, can disperse clouds and stall rain. There were dates when this occurred.

However, the *babalaos* did not meet the Pope during his January 1998 visit, as they had requested. At a news conference in Havana in December 1997, the Bishop of Havana, Jaime Ortega, said that *"sincretismo"* is already part of the Catholic religion in Cuba, and that the Church therefore represents the *babalaos*. *"Sincretismo"* was the approved word for Cuba's mix of Spanish, African, and supposedly native cultures (though no natives are alive today). Santería is another name for a widespread African-origin religion that is called voodoo in Haiti and New Orleans, and macumba in Brazil. As Cuba began to sink into an unmanageable pit of economic despair, Castro's approval of Santería was his version of "voodoo economics." But hidden here was also another agenda: nationalism. The last stage of socialism, as amply proven in Eastern Europe, was nationalism. When all else fails, when everybody is starving, only the call of blood resonates. Nationalism was the tried-and-true last defense of modern tyrants. And nationalism, whether religious or secular, thirsts for only one thing: blood.

The ceremony was taking place at a secret location in Central

Havana. Ariel's husband, Tom, and a German cameraman named Johann had been given the rare privilege of witnessing and recording the ceremony and the sacrifice of a goat. Most ceremonies require no more than a chicken, so this was a big deal.

We piled up into the 1958 Oldsmobile taxi that was to become our official vessel for the next few days, and made our way slowly through the crowded streets of Central Havana. Nineteenth- and eighteenth-century buildings crumbled with tropical abandon. People sat on stones in front of holes that served as makeshift entryways. They were everywhere: thousands of coffee-colored people milling about, looking for somebody to show up.

Our little group tumbled out of the car and was surrounded by begging children. I handed out baseball pencils. The kids started fighting over them. An ancient man pointed us with his head to a dark hall.

The hallway was roofless but paved with star-shaped Spanish tiles in blue, green, and brown, some bright, some faded. I noticed a blackened altar to the left of the entrance. A tiny dwarf-god with cowrie shells around his neck stood in it. The candle drippings at his feet nearly covered him.

Shirtless men in tiny cubicles at the sides were cooking on sooty black stoves. The strong smell of sweat, burning meat, and congealed blood pervaded the tropical heat. At the end of the hall was the *santero*'s hut, its entrance covered with palm fronds. I parted them cautiously and peered inside. A dozen people squatted on the dirt floor in a semicircle around a shirtless middle-aged black man wearing an African hat. He was preaching about the common root of African and Christian belief. "Our Chango," he said, "is angry like Jesus when he whipped the merchants in the Temple. He is soft like a woman when he was punished by God. He loved many women, and they loved him back, like the Magdalene and his holy mother."

There were animal skins on the walls. An altar in the corner was being tended to with incense by a white woman in blue satin hot pants and a tube top, with her back to the *santero*.

"The ceremony is for her," whispered Ariel. "She is here to ask the *santero*'s help to strengthen her mind, because she has a weak mind." I wondered if Ariel meant "weak will," but I saved the question for later. She might well be feebleminded, if she needed a whole goat to set her straight. I had a rather weak mind myself, due to last night's Planter's Poonch. But I liked the sound of the preacher's voice and the attentive heat in the room, though the smell of blood was nauseating. Together with the heat, the sweat, and the incense, it made me swoon. I gagged and backed away from the door. This religion smelled bad: they needed the incense to cover the smell of corpses. Actually, all religions do, and this was another common root.

I backed out of the hut and stood outside, watching an old man fry a piece of liver on a stick over a brick fireplace. Johann, the cameraman, who had already set up his equipment, joined me outside to smoke a cigarette. The heat was frying my brain into something like the stuff on the old man's stick. After a long time, word came from the hut: there would be no goat sacrifice today. Either no goat could be found, or there had been some disagreement with the newspeople over the price. Packing up his gear, Johann told me that he'd been to a ceremony where "seven animals were sacrificed. The smallest was a pigeon, the largest a goat." Of course, killing a cow was worth ten years in the pokey. A pig, one year.

exquisite corpse no. 3

Kill a goat
Kill an hour
Six guns drawn with charcoal heroes
The parrots are driving us crazy
The old thing of power
small man holding the little
power he has been able
to wrest from a beautiful country
that writes sad poetry
Bloated and oozing
Sun and shade, with sharp mirrors.
Hemingway slept here, a fly on his half-drunk *mojito*
until sin is unwritten and laughter banished
el mojito me mojó
& when Hemingway, the last of the *mojitos,* cried
All ends, no means, Justice!

   —Ariel Pena, Tom Gibb, Art Silverman, and Andrei Codrescu
    (December 10, 1997, in the afternoon post-goat-no-show at the Café
    de los Ambos Mundos)

Missing a goat-killing doesn't seem so bad when, soon after, you get to sip a *mojito* at the Cafe de los Ambos Mundos, Hemingway's old haunt in Central Havana. The old bar had lazy ceiling fans, wide leather couches, wide-open louvered doors, a shoeshine stand with an old mulatto sleeping behind it, tiled floors, a boy shaving ice behind the bar, and the best *mojitos* in Havana. It was like Kafka Cafe in Prague, a place ordained for the hangovers of writers. It is said that Old H. wrote *For Whom the Bell Tolls* here. I didn't know about that, but I was sure that he'd *slept* here. I could barely keep my eyes open. I sank deeper and deeper into the cloud-soft couch. I was Our Man in Havana. Graham Greene passed hypnagogically past my lowered eyelids. The bartender had a huge black eye. I half-expected him to say, "H. tried to teach me boxing. He's good." There were rum, mint, limes, ice, sugar, and shaved ice in the *mojito.* It differed from Planter's Poonch in subtle but distinct ways. Aficionados might argue over where the best *mojito* in Havana is made. For my money, Cafe de los Ambos Mundos holds the title. I only had two and they were wildly redolent of literary Cuba. Hemingway, it was said, used to drink six *mojitos* in an afternoon. If so, he was the last of the Mojitos, once a great tribe.

A strolling band—maracas, flute, guitar, and drum—played the "Panadero" (Breadmaker) song. The singer wore a Santeriá necklace. The parrots screeched louder. An eerily blond tourist at the counter was eating a cubano sandwich and noisily gulping hot chocolate. A *mojito*-smashed *jinetera* watched his every slurp like a big, tipsy bird, her hand in his lap.

The distance from Central Havana's slums to Old Havana was psychologically immense. Old Havana, with its sixteenth-century cathedral and its Spanish palaces huddled behind the fortress of El Morro, was rich with history, and protected by the state in the interest of tourism. The cathedral, which had been the scene of plunders, coronations, and orgies, thrust its massive body into the cobblestoned square, dwarfing the cafés and bookstalls doing brisk business in the mind-numbing heat. *Jineteras* hung in clusters before the massive doors, stretching long brown legs out of minimal shorts.

One of the earliest travelers to Cuba, Richard Henry Dana, went to mass here in 1859:

> To the Cathedral, at eight o'clock, to hear mass. . . . Every new eye turns first to the place within the choir, under that

alto-relief, behind that short inscription, where, in the wall of
the chancel, rest the remains of Christopher Columbus. Borne
from Valladolid to Seville, from Seville to San Domingo, and
from San Domingo to Havana, they at last rest here, by the
altar side, in the emporium of the Spanish Islands. "What is
man that thou art mindful of him!" truly and humbly says the
Psalmist; but what is man, indeed, if his fellow men are not
mindful of such a man as this! The creator of a hemisphere![33]

Columbus was gone, the cathedral remained, and the Psalmist had
been right, lo, all these years!

From the exceedingly lazy environs of the downstairs bar we rose
in an ancient art nouveau elevator to the roof terrace for supper. From
up here, we saw Havana spread before us like a multicolored pastel
palm leaf. It stretched into the sea, a jumble of architectures reflecting
decades of decay and prosperity, revolutions, and revolts. The villas of
Vedado, where the Party brass lived, tapered into the crumbling center,
which gave way to the Mafia pleasure palaces of the fifties and then to
Soviet-style apartment buildings that looked prematurely aged. The sea
beat against the wall of the Malecón, the vast promenade full of
strollers at this hour. The sun set over the city, tingeing it in quartz and
gold.

The sounds of a rumba invaded the terrace and four female
dancers in swirling skirts rushed among the tables with soup tureens.
The dancing waitresses were as unexpected as they were vigorous.
They held themselves with balletic grace and shimmied from table to
table, setting down bowls and pouring the milky broth with cauliflower
florets in it without spilling a drop. They were followed by muscular
dancing men, who removed the soup and brought in the second course
of yellow rice, shrimp, and squash. The wine arrived in the hands of yet
another group of dancers, as did rum drinks and mineral water. Six
waves of gorgeous bodies rumba'd and samba'd and flamenco'd their
way through the tables. The effect was magical and surprising and
undiminished by the fact that the show was entirely for the benefit of
tourists. The dancers were the cooks and waitresses of the restaurant,
and called themselves "Ballet Folklórico Culinario."

After dinner, we strolled through the streets. Rusty buses with two
elevated humps, one in front and one in back, barreled by, carrying
squished masses of people. These vehicles were called camels, and they
were one of the few modes of public transport in Havana, the other two

Dancers

being trucks and hitchhiking. Trucks too went by, filled with people packed tightly in the back, holding on to each other. Girls in minidresses and tired women holding meager loaves of bread hitched rides at roadsides. The girls got rides; the women, their faces bitter and stoic, kept waiting, their thumbs rigidly pointed at the flow of old cars and motorcycles. Getting a lift in Havana is called a *"botella."* Ariel speculated that the term, which means "bottle," may refer to shipping out, like a "message in a bottle," but I thought (and didn't say it) that it might have been slang for "penis," a likely hazard to the hitchhiker.

Two huge lines snaked around the block for a Cuban entry in the Havana Film Festival: the movie *El Saffir,* about a group of older (prerevolutionary) Cuban musicians who lived in Miami. A police car issued crowd instructions through a bullhorn, but everybody ignored them. People passed around bottles of rum. The day before, Ariel told me, there'd been a riot at a theater showing the latest Almodóvar movie, because people with film Festival badges got in ahead of ordinary citizens clamoring for seats. It was always like this: mobs contending for the (practically) free cultural fare. Movies cost one peso (nothing). The chewing gum inside costs more than the admission price. It was a policy of circuses—no bread.

Seeing the aimless mobs on the streets, the sardine-packed camel buses, the trucks full of tired people leaving work, the children in miniskirts hitchhiking to get home from school, the people cooking pork skins in overcrowded dilapidated buildings, the proletariat at the cinema, I began to intuit the sadness of this country, the bitterness of the desperately poor masses waiting in a kind of daze for everything. And moving through this world like ghosts, though substantial enough, were the *ideológicos,* the Party commissars, trying to maintain some semblance of the Revolutionary fervor they themselves had long ago ceased believing in. The ineffective policemen with the bullhorn did nothing when the crowd surged before the open doors of the theater. What could they do? They, too, were waiting, like everyone else. The only free things were culture and rum. The sound of the crowd rushing the theater was the clamor of culture in a drunken vacuum.

David and I had a late drink at the National. The band played the "Querido Comandante Che Guevara" song, and the film festival goers twirled on the terrace, visibly more tired than the night before. There was no sign of Julie or Ysemina. Their telephone number had streamed down the sink with the soapy water when I'd washed my hands. I was only a tourist, after all. I hoped, for their sake, that others had kept their number.

"What do you make of this place?" asked David. "Where the hell are the 7-Elevens?"

That will be the day. This soulful and poverty-stricken land was rich in feelings, but you can't eat those. Along the Malecón seawall, there were bodies for sale, and no ships in the harbor. Rumor had it the harbor was mined.

DAY THREE: "THIS CORPSE IS CALLED LA LUCHA"

On the Malecón

exquisite corpse no. 4

This corpse is called La Lucha*
just too skinny
Slender, tender talk
chicken slapping
I escaped from my bosses
& got hung up on liberty
& had to listen to the Che Guevara song
one hundred times
Globes floating among the palms
A Zombie, a cactus, a crystal & the eye of a camel
One, two, three, and all of them forget dreams
I'm done, we're you, let's eat

—Art Silverman, Ariel Pena, David Graham, Tom Gibb, and Pat Flynn† (December 11, 1997)

---

*La Lucha, or "The Struggle," is the term used by Castro to denote the difficult times the Cubans are experiencing after the collapse of the Soviet Union. La Lucha called the people to make greater sacrifices to save the Revolution.
†Pat Flynn, producer for PBS, who joined us on the terrace at the National for this poem. Pat took Art's audiotapes and some of my notes with her when she left the country because we were afraid, after an incident I will recall later, that the police might confiscate our materials.

PABLO

In front of the Capri, the *jineteros* were thick, more *jineteros* than *jineteras* this time, maybe because the girls worked in the daytime in offices and factories. When we exited the Capri, two skinny kids accosted us. One of them spoke English: "Where are you from? Spain? Italy? Estados Unidos? Wow! My dad is a Marielito—he lives in Miami. We talk on the phone. My English pretty good, no? You like my English? I go to tourism school. That man"—long-beard gesture—"is crazy. He drive us all crazy. You don't how poor is poor. You want to see a Cuban market? Shit. You want to see the girl place? The drug place? The church place?"

Art and David were ignoring the *jinetero*, but I was interested. His English really was pretty good, and his nonstop patter was full of nuggets of articulate social criticism. He had a gold tooth that flashed in his intelligent-looking chocolate face like a lighthouse signal. He said his name was Pablo, and that his friend was Luis. I shook their hands.

"Things will be shit for another twenty years," Pablo said, and made the air-beard gesture again. I handed him and his friend Luis some money and some of my baseball pencils. Pablo refused at first, then said: "You have to come to my house, you have to see how Luis lives. Real Cuba. Not that propaganda."

We were walking along, David snapping pictures, Art taping street sounds, the *jineteros* hot on our heels.

Pablo said: "Cubans have a lot of rights. You know what they are? Education, health, housing, and stealing from the state."

I laughed. Our second Cuban joke.

Pablo pointed to a camel-bus with people hanging outside from the door. "Crazy transport. I go in there, I steal something from somebody, somebody steals something from me. By the time you get off, you stole your stuff back."

I wasn't sure this was a joke, but I thought, "Third joke," anyway.

After some hesitation by my companions (Ariel was not with us this morning), I decided that we ought to take Pablo up on his offer to show us where he lives, the "real Cuba." If this had been New York and a fast-talking hustler had decided to take us to, let's say, Harlem, I might have had second thoughts. But I'd heard that Cuba had little violent crime (a claim rejected later, emphatically, by people who knew) and decided to take a chance.

The section of Central Havana where the taxi deposited the five of us was even more sinister looking than the missed-goat neighborhood. It was a maze of ruins of nineteenth-century buildings that once must have looked Parisian. They were called *solares,* because they were mostly roofless and the tropical sun came in unobstructed. Up to ten people lived in each one-room apartment. Every entrance twisted into a dark alley leading to makeshift cubicles, rickety stairs. Shirtless men cooked on ancient gas stoves, women nursed babies under the glow of small TVs, toothless old people mumbled in the dark.

Luis and Pablo's one-room home stank like frying fat, pigs, chickens, and shit. It opened into a small cement courtyard overhung with laundry. A roofless kitchen was at the end. Fat bubbled in a pot.

"You want to see the bathroom?" Pablo grinned with inexplicable delight. I took one look at the foul-smelling hole in the ground with a bucket next to it and beat a retreat. We were introduced to Pablo's mother and grandmother, and an angry-looking teenager. A baby who was either asleep or dead—he didn't stir during the entire visit—lay in a stroller covered up. Pablo said, "It's my baby, his mother is Luis's sister, she's here somewhere."

She appeared later, a tough-looking teenager, and said, "I'm taking the baby to the doctor." But an hour later, the baby was still there, the mother nowhere in sight.

I interviewed Pablo by the boiling clothes in the back. I asked him how the family survived.

"You have six pounds of rice a month. A few pounds of sugar. No potatoes. Eggs, you know. We have seven eggs a month. Milk is only for children to seven years old, you know."

"So what do you do about that?"

"We go into the street, talk to the tourist. We try to live, without fooling the tourist."

I had my doubts about this, but let it pass.

"The girls are out there working," I said.

"We are in trouble. They sells their body. They don't know what they do. You go on the Malecón Avenue at nine o'clock. You see the girls. Yes, we have problems, we have no money, nothing to do, you know?"

"You're speaking honestly."

"I'm not afraid. Many things we can't talk about. We only have two TV channels, only the communist newspaper. They speak a lot of shits about the U.S.A."

"Do most young people feel the way you do?"

"Ninety percent do. Only the old people who fought in Revolution feel other. But nothing gonna change, nothing gonna happen. In kindergarten we sang songs about the Revolution." Pablo pulled out his wallet and showed me his ID. "This is when you were born, your mother, your photo, and here it says, 'Skin color, *mulato*.' That's all who I am."

"Your skin. I thought your color didn't matter in Cuba."

"It's lies. Black is poor."

"What are you going to do?"

"Get the hell out of this country. Everybody wants to. We look at the water every day. Every day I see a boat, a tire, a piece of wood . . . out of here."

Pablo was a gumbo of bravura and contradictions, and I had a feeling that we were nowhere near the bottom of the pot. Politics was, of course, one commodity. Another was about to appear.

"You want to buy cigars? Luis's uncle steals them from the factory direct."

"How much are these cigars?" David asked. He was interested. He was getting quite a taste for Cuban cigars.

"It depends how many boxes you going to buy. If you buy five boxes, maybe the price is going down. We try to live. It's like *paladares*, you know."

Paladares were the new private businesses allowed in Cuba. Small restaurants, tiny hotels. The restaurants were allowed only five tables, and were forbidden to serve beef, shrimp, or lobster, which were state monopolies. The hotels were also restricted to five rooms and couldn't serve food. But licensed *paladares* paid half their earnings to the government. I doubted that Pablo had any such intentions.

"Okay. Let me see the Monte Cristos."

Luis disappeared through a hole in the back wall and was gone for about twenty minutes. During that time we crouched in the dark room, flies buzzing around us, the baby not moving. The sound of fights, broken glass, and a baseball game on the radio provided Pablo with background for his nonstop patter. His subject was Cuba, and he wanted us to know all about it, because he thought about it all the time.

"All these people crowded here are from Oriente, the East. People here in Havana hate these people from Santiago, it's like Bosnia and Herzegovina, we call them Palestinians." There are no precise figures on how many people are now living illegally in Havana, but some estimates put the number of "*palestinos*" at 400,000.[34]

Over and over, Pablo returned to the Bearded One, whose name he never mentioned, only making the beard sign with his hand. After a particularly inspired diatribe, he fell silent for a brief moment, then mused, in flagrant contradiction to what he'd just said: "He's not a bad guy, you know. He wants the best for Cuba. But you know who stops him?"

I had an idea.

"The communists! If he could, he would. But the communists, they criminals."

I wondered just how magnetic Fidel's draw must be if, after all these years, he still managed to somehow project himself outside the system he'd created. But Pablo wasn't wrong, In his speeches, Fidel cleverly blamed the Party for failures, and hinted that things might have been different if his authority had been unhindered.

Luis returned with four beautiful boxes. In the stark room, the cigars shone incongruously in their luxurious silver tubes. David admired their individual cedar-leaf wrappings and inhaled their deep, fine tobacco aroma. A beautiful box of Romeo y Julietas beckoned to him. Luis had labels, too, to glue the boxes shut so they looked factory-new. He also provided a receipt he insisted would keep the Cubans from confiscating them at the border.

"These are three hundred dollars at the store!" exclaimed Pablo. We worked out a $120 price and the box of twenty-five was ours. This transaction, of course, was precisely the kind of thing every guidebook advises against. Do not buy cigars on the street, they warn, they are phony. But David swore that they were just fine. Only later, when we actually bought some from the cigar factory, the same box was $25. This was one of the many ways in which our fixer, Pablo, worked out his fee. But it was worth it.

After the cigar deal, I thought that our adventure in the bowels of Havana might end. But I was very wrong. Pablo said, "Do you want to go the church place? My uncle Miguel El Gordo is a famous *santero*, a *babalao*."

In for a penny, in for a pound.

Santería

Kill a chicken
Kill an hour
Six guns drawn with charcoal heroes
The parrots are driving us crazy
The old thing of power

small man holding the little
power he had been able
to gather in a tin cup
A beautiful country writes sad poetry
Bloated and oozing
Sun and shade, with sharp mirrors.

—by Ariel Pena, Tom Gibb, Art Silverman, and Andrei Codrescu

The church place was on the terrace of a four-story *solario*. We climbed the twisted staircase, past a huge pig tied to an outdoor bathtub. A tattooed guy with a black eye who looked like he'd just escaped from prison crossed his arms across his bare chest and watched us go by. He smelled like rum and murder, and I didn't blame him. A skin-and-bones woman in a dirty yellow slip, with bruises all over her legs, was hanging what looked like his dress jeans on a clothesline strung between a broken window and a telephone pole. The pig must have been theirs; it looked like part of the family.

"How did they get the pig up here?" I asked Art.

"Like the pear in the bottle." Art was one tough *hombre*.

The *babalao* lived one floor above, with what I assumed to be his father, his three uncles, three aunts, a wife, and a variety of naked children, one of which was feeding on the breast of a fifteen-year-old girl. His name was Miguel El Gordo ("the Fat"), but he wasn't that fat, only a bit thicker than the rest of his undernourished tribe. He did turn out to have high blood pressure, as we found out when he offered Art a swig of rum and Art refused, citing his high blood pressure. Miguel El Gordo offered that he, too, had high blood pressure, and he engaged Art in a long discussion about this condition. He was interested in medicine for it, and Art promised to send him some. Santería didn't cure everything, it seems. Miguel was Pablo's uncle.

Pablo, it turned out, was learning to be a *babalao* himself. He knew his way around the rituals. He pointed out a variety of clay jars and stones lined on shelves against the walls of the small room. Inside these lived the *orishas*, the gods. There was Obatala, the King of the White Cloth, father of humanity, identified with Jesus Christ; Orunla, the patron saint of the *babalao*, the diviner of the gods and the owner of the Table of Ifa, the major divination system of the *santeros*; Babalu-Aye, who was also St. Lazarus, and who could either heal or bring about dreadful diseases from cancer to syphilis to leprosy to paralysis, and other afflictions; Oggun, the patron of metals and metallurgy; Chango, the god of fire, lightning, and sexuality, who could change sex at will and was also Santa Barbara in the Catholic Church. Every Santería god has an equivalent Catholic saint. Each has a multitude of aspects and rules over specific parts of the body, emotions, and elements. The jurisdiction of Oshun, the love goddess, for instance, stretched over all matters of the heart. Oshun also controlled children, money, pleasures, and the river waters. She was identified with the Virgen de la Caridad del Cobre, the patron saint of Cuba.

Pablo was solemn, professorial almost, as he pointed out the gods. There was reverence as he bowed slightly, though he never lost his hustler cool. The *orishas*, he said, were a complex and lengthy subject of study, taking many years. Initiations were costly and rigorous. Miguel was Pablo's *padrino*, or godfather, and ruled his life. The others, whom I had first mistaken for a natural family, were actually disciples who were learning to be *santeros*.

Everyone crowded in a circle to hear my fortune told. I wasn't sure I wanted to hear it. I find soothsaying distressing because, right or wrong, it points out the depressing similarity of all human situations. An astute observer can easily discern the patterns of a life and make you tremble before the obvious. It is bad enough when you are alone with the diviner. But when there are ten people looking on, plus your amused producer and photographer, the discomfort may be considerable. It was. Nonetheless, in the grip of general curiosity, I took the bait.

Babalao Miguel sat on a three-legged stool and I crouched on the ground before him. He handed me two smooth black stones to hold in my hands, then closed his eyes and started chanting. He stopped abruptly after a few minutes, removed a strand of cowrie shells from around his neck, and threw them at my feet. The necklace uncoiled like a snake, startling me, and I gripped the black stones tighter. Miguel chanted and threw the necklace several times. Each time he picked it up he read out loud the markings, and an old man wrote down the symbols on a torn paper bag. He wrote in vertical columns. I figured this was something like the I Ching, where the combinations tell the story.

After Miguel took the sweaty stones from my hand, the old man read the symbols he had written down. The *babalao* listened with his eyes closed, then opened them and said: "The *orishas* have spoken!"

Pablo translated this, then everyone looked at Miguel, who pushed up his stomach and began to deliver the *orishas'* message:

"Ugh, ugh," he said in Spanish, and Pablo translated: "You have very hard enemies, you know. Take care. You need to care who you give your reports. And if you have divorce, you need to take care."

"I see. So I have to watch out."

Miguel *y* Pablo: "The people hate you, but I don't know why, 'cause you're a very good guy, you know."

"You're right, I'm a good guy."

Pablo translated "You're right," and all the ten heads watching bobbed up and down with delight and pride in their *santero*.

"But I don't think people hate me."

Hmm. Miguel was thoughtful. "You have no religion?"

"Not really."

"You have no reason for doing, no hope?"

"No, no, I like my work."

"For the money."

"No, no, I do it from the heart."

I think Miguel was going generic here. I'm American, and everyone knows that Americans do things for money. Not Cubans, of course.

"No," I said again, firmly, "I do things because I want to."

The heads looked distressed.

"You need to change the house."

"You are right about that."

Happiness reigned once more. The heads smiled, nodded approvingly. Miguel had rehabilitated himself. He threw the shells again and called out their names.

"You are going clean to your country and all the bad things stay here in Cuba. You leave the bad things here."

"Okay. So, to clear my head, I need to leave the bad things here. Aren't there enough bad things in Cuba? Do I need to add mine?"

Everybody laughed at this, but not Miguel. "Cubans have lots of problems, but try to make life better with religion."

"Religion makes things better, makes me clean?"

"You need to clean everything. All the bad things. You need to take care with your elimination. You need to take care with your testicles. Don't cover your nose when you sleep. You leave the drink, you know. You need to leave the drink a little bit. Because it have very bad problems with your stomach."

"That's right," I said. "My father had problems with his stomach. That's why he died."

Everyone nodded at this, and two uncles slapped hands.

"Need to give ceremony for your father. You have to give food to the spirit of your father. You know. The spirit of your father lives with you."

I understood Miguel's Spanish perfectly, and I spoke to him directly, though Pablo kept translating.

"This is very good for me," I said. "I feel the energy in this room, and I'm very grateful to you." It was the truth. The room felt sparklingly alive and Miguel's words had found their target. I *did* need to lay off the whiskey. Drink *did* kill my father. I suddenly didn't care who was in the room. I was ready to do whatever the man said.

"We need to buy a chicken," Pablo said. "Give him ten bucks. He going for the chicken, okay?"

I had hoped to see a Santería ceremony but I'd had no idea that I'd end up the subject. There had been a reason why that goat hadn't been killed the day before. Once you start thinking like this, magically, everything makes sense. Too much sense. I knew also, from previous encounters with psychics, that I was an easy mark. Pass a hand over my eyes and I go under like a fish.

One of Miguel's kin went for the chicken. "Ten bucks for a chicken?" whispered David.

"If it works, it's cheap." Last time I'd let myself be worked on by a psychic I'd saved months of psychotherapy.

We walked outside on the roof terrace and the light was blinding. The noon heat was intense. I put on my shades. Most of the men, including the *babalao*, were shirtless. The children were naked, and the women wore wraparound skirts, with kerchiefs around their breasts. The rooftops of central Havana looked like a breezy harbor full of sails. Everyone's laundry was dancing in the wind. I could see nearly nude people lounging, smoking, and listening to radios. Pigs and dogs lay before them, and parrots perched on homemade TV antennas. The smell of frying bananas and fish saturated the air.

A few minutes later Miguel's man returned with a pretty little rooster with many-colored feathers. The rooster was squawking mightily, surely aware of what awaited him. Miguel took him firmly by the legs and swung him in a circle.

I said: "He knows what's happening. This is one chicken who seems incredibly conscious of the fact it's going to be sacrificed momentarily for my health, so that I will get rid of all the bad things and leave them in Cuba."

Miguel donned a robe with an African pattern. He bowed before an altar I hadn't noticed, at the far right of the terrace. It was a blackened barbecue pit made of bricks, with caked blood on it. He asked me to remove my shirt and turn my back to him. The whole family gathered behind Miguel. I took off my shirt, and Pablo laughed. "You sure are a white man."

I felt white. What's more, I became incredibly self-conscious about my white American belly, which stuck out among all these skinny Cubans like the lid of a silver tureen hiding Yankee bounty. I vowed to get rid of it.

Chanting started up behind me, a strange polyrhythmic recitation in Yoruba. I heard the name "Oshun" over and over. And "Obatala." I closed my eyes. I was in Africa. The chanting grew and grew in intensity, making me feel light. The heat was penetrating every pore, and I was pouring sweat. The chanting stopped abruptly and the *babalao* commanded loudly: *"What's your name?"*

"Andrei Codrescu."

"LOUDER!"

"ANDREI CODRESCU. CO-DRESS-COU."

"WHICH ONE THE OTHER NAME?"

"That's all I have. Andrei Codrescu. I'm poor, I have only two names."

The *babalao* shouted out a rendition of my name, a strangely inflected Afro-Cuban sound. The chicken cried anxiously. I closed my eyes again, only to open them in shock when I felt a jet of rum spat onto my back. Miguel took mouthfuls of rum and spat them on everybody, including David and Art.

Just as I got a bit used to the rivulets of hot alcohol pouring down my sweaty skin, I felt the soft touch of feathers on my midriff. Then there were feathers on my neck. Miguel was passing the rooster over my whole body. It was only a light caress at first, but then he swung it harder, and the terrified chicken let out some awful squawks and started scratching me with his beak. I could feel him drawing blood all over my back and shoulders. And then Miguel placed the chicken on my head, after which he took a couple of steps back and started swinging hard and beating me with it across my whole bloody, sweating, feather-covered, naked torso. The blood and sweat were really pouring by then and I had the scary thought that he was going to beat the little bird to death on me. The chanting had meanwhile ascended to a roar and Oshun's name was being called loud enough to wake him from whatever god-jar he'd been slumbering in. The *santero* withdrew the rooster suddenly. I felt the presence of something chilly and velvety, and I got goosebumps. Then the chanting stopped. I turned around and saw the rooster, dead for my sins, full of all the bad things in my body, lying pathetically at Miguel's feet in a pool of blood, his neck severed and his head barely hanging on to his pretty little body. The sad little cock-a-doodle lay very quiet and very dead. I sure hoped he'd make a fine soup, my sins notwithstanding.

As I put my shirt back on, Pablo whispered: "Give money to Oshun," and pointed to the altar.

"How much?"

"About thirty dollars."

I laid down about fifteen on the blood-spattered brick.

After that, Miguel went inside, changed his shirt, and came out with a fresh bottle of rum and little glasses. He poured us each one and we clinked, toasting to everyone's health. I felt quite good—oddly light-hearted, actually.

"Do you know what that ceremony was for?" asked Miguel. Pablo translated. "For your father. For his freedom. He like you very much. He now don't worry. He go away to higher spirit world."

My poor father, dead so many years ago. I doubted very much he'd hung around all this time in spirit form to see how I was doing, He'd hung around no longer than six months when he was alive—what would have caused him to do so for thirty years after he died? But who knows? I don't often think of my father, but sitting there in the tropical heat on a slum roof drinking rum with Cuban spirit workers, nothing seemed impossible. I felt actually some pity for the man, thought kindly of him even, and something left me, making me feel lighter.

After we were through with my father, we talked about Fidel. Miguel confirmed that the *santeros* think that he is a saint. They reserved a place of honor for his image among the saints of Santería and of the Catholic Church.

I asked Miguel, "What will happen when Castro dies?" But it was Pablo who answered: "Something more bad than him going to be." Miguel looked wistfully at Pablo, then shook his head. "Young people! Many bosses are more bad. But Fidel Castro is okay. He have many good things."

We shook hands with everyone and felt genuine regret in parting. I had liked them all.

After we regained the street, past the goon with crossed arms and the tied-up pig and the twisted narrow stone staircase, Pablo asked: "Do you want to see private market where chicken come from?"

He took us down some alley at the end of which a sorry assortment of rickety tables held shriveled black bananas, some grotesquely huge manioc roots, piles of little potatoes. A man was butchering an animal and dropping bloody hunks of meat on a dirty stone table. Swarms of flies buzzed over it and a crowd clamored like the flies around the meat, but nobody was buying.

"Dollars," said Pablo, "all cost dollars. Nobody has dollars."

The private markets, Pablo explained, were run by the army, which alone had the trucks to transport the peasants and their produce to city markets. In exchange, they got half the profits. In addition to being in private business, Castro's army, the largest standing army in Latin America, was well fed compared to the rest of the people. The soldiers had no need for clothes, either, since they wore state-issued uniforms. A military business-state might well follow socialism in Cuba.

I thanked Pablo for the tour of his world. I was anxious to get back to the hotel to take a shower and wash the blood, sweat, and feathers off. The rooster's scratches were stinging. Pablo was astounded at this early departure. "This is only beginning. I show you more Cuba. You want to go to drug place? Marijuana? Cocaína? Heroin? We have all in Havana. I show you the girls, the boys, what you like."

It was hard convincing him that we soft Yankees cannot endure too many sensations all at once. I slipped him forty dollars, but he waved my hand away. "Now we see really interesting things." I insisted he take the money and, finally, he did. We shook hands. Pablo looked gloomily down the crowded street and shrugged, looking older than his nineteen years. "Okay," he said, "you go sleep. I go have sex. Maybe a woman, maybe a man. Maybe I come, maybe not. We Cubans like fuck a lot."

He seemed disappointed by our prudishness. Actually, I wanted to go along. A good thing Art and David were there.

In the shower later, I poured half a bottle of rum on my scratches. They stung like hell. My chest had actual chicken scratches. Not a girl—a chicken! As the tepid water washed the feathers, blood, dirt, and sweat off my body, I thought that if Pablo had been living in Miami, he'd have had an office and a cell phone. What would have been a true price for a tour like this? There was no American equivalent of such experiences.

Pablo did find us again, next evening, and we did pay, though not much. He and Luis captured us by the doors of the Capri and took us to eat fish, black beans, rice, and fruit salad, and drink beer in an empty private restaurant, a *paladar* called El Sagitario. The check for the meal for four was ninety-five dollars. Not bad for Washington, D.C., but four times as much as any other meal in Cuba. Pablo's cut, I figure, was forty dollars. We wrote a corpse:

exquisite corpse no. 5

Cuba fruit cocktail
Odors or other entertainments
For freedom is all the man need
Me gusta las nuferes
Fish, chicken, religion, metal on flesh
Skinny young girls with bouncy tits
Some do, some sing about it
The best part of time the girls
are very satisfying very important
Me gusta todos

—Pablo, Luis, Art, David, and Andrei

The cigars we'd bought from Pablo were cheaper at the factory, so throw in a ten-dollar cigar commission. Maybe, too, he got a cut from the purchase of the ten-dollar chicken that was sacrificed for me. Maybe Pablo cleared sixty bucks. Not bad in dollar-hungry Cuba, but disproportionate to Pablo's talents, which, somewhere else, might have made him a millionaire by now. I admired him, even as I realized that Pablo might have also been working for the police, just as hustlers in Ceaușescu's Romania did. It was just a feeling.

"How do you stay away from the police?" I asked him.

He laughed. "The police has to live, man. You give him a dollar." Then he became wistful. "Not always. Me and Luis went to jail maybe six times. Everybody go to jail. If I buy at the private market, come home with the package of maybe meat for my mother, milk for the baby, the policeman ask for receipt. No receipt, he take you to jail. You give him money, he take the package, bastard still take you to jail."

And would I have followed this charmer into the bowels of a slum in, let's say, New York or Marseilles? Probably not. In Cuba, at least for now, you are more likely to be cured of your ills by a voodoo priest than end up with a knife in your back.

Before we parted again, I asked him: "What do you think you'll be doing in the future? Do you have plans for the future?"

"In all the ways, take off from Cuba, you know? I don't want to live in Cuba. If Cuba change, you need a lot of money to make something, make some business. Make something. In many ways, we need to take off. Here will be crazy. Maybe we have war inside. I don't know. I don't want to stay here, okay? It's my opinion. I don't know other people. I'm not too intelligent, but I try to be intelligent, you know? I try to learn in life. Not everything is the money, but we need the money. For that reason, you need to take off. Because people without money are nothing. You can see. It's crazy." He laughed again, a laugh too wise for his years.

It was crazy, all right: Not everything is money. People without money are nothing. Has anyone put it better? Pablo surely was one of a kind. But I had the feeling the slums of Cuba teemed with young men who thought the way he did.

This was Cuba now: poised precariously between the lost utopia and the unpolished hustle.

Meat!

DAY FOUR: "I WAS IN ARREARS TO MY BAD PERSONA"

exquisite corpse no. 6

I was in arrears to my bad persona
at the *nomenklatura* restaurant.
Marbled fans plowing condensed air
across worries—
Dance if you see the shadows.
I discovered a space, another
one to attach to the previous
one that I discovered—
Fidel's poodles play upon the people
and Fidel is a great party guy
with gas, not—
The fourth parliament
went on to Casablanca.

> **—Ariel Pena, Art Silverman, David Graham, and Andrei Codrescu (at Paladar de Lillian)**

We rose on the morning of the twelfth without hangovers. We had our breakfast of papaya, bananas, oranges, one ripe mango, café con leche and grapefruit juice, and poked our heads outside for the weather. Clouds were rolling in over the sea and the Malecón was being battered by waves that spumed over the top of it. Thunder rumbled somewhere. A vendor agreed to sell me *Granma*. There are no newsstands in Cuba, therefore no newspapers or magazines. *Granma*, the only daily, is hawked by street vendors for a very short time in the morning, and it's usually gone by nine a.m. And, of course, you have to be an iron-willed ascetic with a commie-speak decoder to get through *Granma*'s lingo sludge. Nonetheless, I looked at it, pretending that it was a real news-paper. The lead story was "Sugar Harvest Priority: Efficiency and Lower Costs." Now, there was something to think about. The night before, I'd watched the half-hour Nightly News. Over a soothing soundtrack, fields of sugar cane rolled gently. The caption over this idyllic Sominex-scape was "Sugar Harvest's Priority: Efficiency and Lower Costs." And now here it was, in print, just in case I'd missed it. Who needs *The New York Times*? There were other publications in Cuba, but they went directly to their targeted constituencies. *Juventud Rebelde,* for instance, was directed to Communist youth, and featured anti-U.S. diatribes that listed in order all our sins: racism, violence, drug use, the government's treatment of Native Americans.

While waiting for Ariel, I had another cup of coffee, a Cuban espresso this time, at the corner bar. David and Art had mineral waters. When I looked idly over the lobby, I beheld a heart-stopping sight. I saw my childhood.

Three angelic Pioneers with well-ironed red neckerchiefs looked at the brand-new and newly permitted Christmas tree under the watchful gaze of a teacher. One of the girls held herself like a ballerina, with breathtaking sweetness, a future Alicia Alonso. After they looked at the Christmas tree they sat quietly on a couch, waiting for their teacher, who was having an animated conversation with a blond woman who worked at the hotel.

Oh, happy commie childhood! I remembered being a contented Pioneer, safe in the cocoon of the state, protected from the nasty news of the real world, warm in the embrace of Stalin, my true father. Stalin's mustache, like Castro's beard, watched over my childhood, a horizon of security. Socialism had made it similarly safe for children in places as dissimilar as Romania and Cuba. Thousands of years of climate, temperament, language, physiognomy, and social organization were wiped out by a few decades of the socialist experiment, and certainly out of our childhoods. To this day, despite their cries of nationalist anguish, Romanians of my generation have more in common with Bulgarians, Mongolians, and Cubans of the same age than with our ancestors. Our similarities aren't just cosmetic, like slogans on walls, red neckerchiefs, or the "Internationale." They go deeper down, almost to the reptilian brain where the oldest reflexes are. Something Pavlovian was involved in our construction. By reassuring the people, especially children, that we lived in Paradise, the commies induced the old reptilian brain to respond positively, sweeping aside some of the more fanciful products of the neocortex, such as tribal identity and cultural difference. Of course, the last stage of socialism, just before collapse— and Cuba was no exception—was the return of an atavistic nationalism, which lay just below the thin skin of Paradise. In the end, the pseudoscientific utopia turned out to be only the topmost layer. Below that were the memories and passions of our parents and grandparents with their threads of national pride and the constructions of historical identity. In Romania now, the rhetorical topsoil of communism had been blown away like so much tired cowshit, revealing, beneath, the blood-soaked soil that oozed there all along. Still: what comfort there was in the illusion of my protected childhood! Growing up fatherless after the war, like so many of my contemporaries, I believed wholeheartedly in the *über*-father. Stalin and Castro and all the rest of them provided the children of the postwar, postrevolution, postslaughter with an astounding normality. False, of course, like all perfect fairy tales. And now here they were: Raúl Estevez Sardina, age ten, Maureen Cil García, age ten, and Heidy Batista García, age ten. And their teacher was Thislée Cleta Calderón, one of the most beautiful names I have ever heard. Say that, classically: Thislée Cleta Calderón.

One of the advantages of living in a world without newspapers is that you can be a happy commie Boy Scout—though I must say that these three were *good* Pioneers, while I was bad. My neckerchief never looked as whole as theirs. I chewed mine all the way to the knot. The anxiety that made me gnaw my socialist cravat must have been the suspicion that all was not what it seemed.

The drawbacks of knowledge are infinite. I also knew, in an undefinable way, that the blond woman who'd been conversing with the nice teacher was some kind of cop.

HAVANA, Jan. 2, 1998 (Associated Press)—Cuba is cutting pants to cut costs, declaring that it is replacing schoolboys' slacks with shorts to save cloth. Cuban fifth and sixth graders soon will be issued Bermuda shorts, with hems hitting just below the knees, the communist government said this week.

Pioneers at the Capri

The Communist Party daily Granma said the measure would allow the government to produce 28,000 more school uniforms for Cuban children for the 1998–1999 school year. Younger boys receive shorts and older boys wear long pants. Girls wear culottes.

What's next? Pioneer cravats? Never. *No pasaran.*

Ariel arrived just in time to save me from giving myself over to the despair of knowing too much. She had news. Mario Coyula, the planner of the city of Havana and the right-hand man to Eusebio Leal, had agreed to see us. It was rumored that Eusebio Leal, the chief architect of the city of Havana, was the third or fourth most powerful man in Cuba. We had heard that Eusebio Leal's office demanded five hundred dollars for an interview, so we'd settled for the younger Coyula, whose influence was also said to be considerable. (In the next few days we did make more attempts to see Eusebio Leal, and he did finally agree [waiving the fee], but by that time we had other plans.

MARIO COYULA

Mario Coyula's office was in a villa-sized modern building in a middle-class section of the city. His receptionist sent us to a patio in the back, by an empty swimming pool. We sat in some metal bucket seats by a small table. Power in Cuba was not ostentatious. The powerful are anonymous and their offices are modest. Their boss is famous enough for all of them. I once asked Tom Gibb if he knew all the faces crowded behind Castro in a photograph at some congress or other. Tom said, yes, but it had taken him ten years.

Cuban children

Coyula was a handsome, affable man, with the world-weary look of a progressive intellectual. As we shook hands, I was reminded of certain Romanian dissidents of the pre-1989 era, reformers who thought that they were going to change communism from within, either by giving it a "human face" or by putting a suit on it. Coyula wore a nice

Cuban children

suit, but his tie was a bit askew, as befits a visionary. His English was perfect, even a bit American-hip. He'd been to academic conferences in the United States.

I asked him if the city of Havana was lucky to have so many great buildings.

"Every problem brings new solutions. It's a matter of choosing, making trade-offs. Truth can change in time."

Which meant, I believe, that the wealth was a mixed blessing. Eighty old buildings fall down in Havana every year. Estimated costs for reversing the decay were around $30 billion just for Old Havana. Mario Coyula listed Havana's architectural periods: "We have buildings from the sixteenth century. Then the pre-baroque buildings from the seventeenth century, with Spanish-Moorish influence, and shipbuilding influence. If you notice, early 1600s buildings are like inverted ship hulls. Then we had baroque, but styles settled in Cuba very slowly. This was quite late baroque, mid- and late eighteenth century. Then in the early nineteenth century, we had the neoclassical style, and increasing French influence. Then we had thirty years of independence wars that practically destroyed the country. Building was paralyzed. Then four years of American intervention that created the base infrastructure, sewers, paved streets. This was very important, for the next construction boom during the First World War. Big boom in the eclectic, but it arrived too late in Cuba. We had art deco, too. Geometric style, then we had a very strong modern movement up to the mid-sixties. Then the noncultural approach, that was a disaster. Huge housing tracts. There was a short modern architectural period in the late eighties. It was not terribly relevant. We have this huge heritage, an affluent city by Latin American standards. But now the city is dilapidated, overcrowded. Public spaces are not good. It isn't just a matter of maintenance, but of behavior."

This was a fine lesson in history that brought us right into the present. Coyula's candor surprised me. Calling the Soviet era "the noncultural approach" might sound mild to American ears, but it was a pretty strong condemnation. The centerpiece of that epoch was the huge housing development at Alomar, Castro's pride and joy for many years, his favorite place to show foreign journalists. Alomar had been built by the workers themselves, and had been a dream come true for many immigrants from the eastern provinces to Havana. Castro liked to drop in unexpectedly (with reporters in tow) on Alomar families, who reacted as if they'd expected him and were overjoyed. The clean children, the new classrooms, the kitchens with refrigerators—all these things made Alomar the propaganda flagship of socialism. That had been before the collapse of public transportation in the nineties, the blackouts, food rationing, and the quick physical decay of the buildings themselves, which had been built in a hurry from shoddy materials.

Mario Coyula didn't pull any punches. "The development houses one hundred thousand people. There are no jobs out there. There's no proper transportation. If buses were regular, the bus trip would take twenty minutes. The approach was supposed to be that the only way to deal with two hundred years of history was in opposition, that if you wanted to meet the needs, you would have to sacrifice beauty. Very naive thinking. Obviously, you can do great architecture with few materials. A palm thatch hut can be beautiful. But we were convinced this was the way. Many of the new buildings were made from prefabricated materials that left no places for water to run out, so now they are being destroyed by humidity."

There was a hint of mea culpa here. He'd said, "We were convinced . . . ," and we knew that once he had been. But he looked toward the future.

"Demolish the projects? Raze Central Havana?" I asked.

"Depends what standards you want. We'll never bring them to the standards of a U.S. yuppie." Mario pronounced this "yoopie." "The only way to preserve the city is to make it pay for itself."

Whoa. We were far from socialism here. Was this man a dangerous radical? "Foreign investment is needed."

"Is there debate about privatization?" I wanted to know just how widespread this capitalist urge was.

"It's practically the only way to bring money, but it creates problems. It's a matter of balance. I don't like gentrification. But we need to attract more affluent people. On the other hand, we should stimulate the local economy. Maybe have neighbors' cooperatives. The government should run the country, but not administrate everything. It's silly to think that the state should administrate enterprises like soft drinks. It's stupid. Surviving is not enough. Some people think hard times are just to survive. But we should learn a lesson from hard times. In everything there should be a lesson to learn about."

Incendiary speech. Adroit speech. I looked around. The banana tree shook off a couple of microphones. On the one hand, I was sure that the questions of investment and capitalism had been debated intensely at the top level of the Communist Party, and that Mario Coyula had been at the forefront of the pro-investment side. On the other hand, his vehemence pointed also to the possibility that he might lose the battle, depending on who inherited Cuba from Castro. If Mario and his side won, they would be the leaders of post-Castro Cuba. If Raúl Castro or any of the pro-Chinese leadership did, Mario would be in hot water. On yet another hand (the third hand), Mario made sure that his allegiance to a rational (read: Marxist) view of the world was noted. Privatization, he implied, was an objective necessity, inevitable. Everything was dialectical, hence part of the struggle: lessons must be learned from conditions. He was also wily enough not to propose dismantling the state: "Of course, the major industries, coal, electricity, transportation, must remain in the hands of the state. I am talking about small private enterprise, and foreign investment. . . ."

Was he backtracking? Not at all. He was advocating a third way between socialism and capitalism, like the gorbachevists of yesteryear. Was he aware that such a third way was impossible? That it hadn't worked at all? That once the wedge of capitalism was in, the whole shithouse fell down in a hurry? There are few gorbachevists left in Russia or Eastern Europe now. There are an awful lot of disappointed, enlightened, and disgusted intellectuals, though, people like Mario Coyula who now draw miserable salaries from the universities where they teach, wondering where their dreams of reform went.

Mario now invited us to follow him inside. We walked into an extraordinary room, a domed hall the entire surface of which was taken up by an elevated, three-dimensional scale model of the city of Havana. There it was, the whole mighty product of five centuries of the history of the New World. Though still unfinished, the model was accurate in every detail. Every house, church, monument, and shop in the city was there, down to the tiniest features. A millimeter-tall man would have been in the real place.

"The model is one to a thousand. One meter is one kilometer. We have one hundred square meters already. All the most important parts of the city. . . . The waterfront is complete. . . . When we are done, the model will be one hundred and forty-four square meters total."

Mario pointed out various areas of the city with a red laser light, explaining what was important, what should be demolished, what restored, what left alone. He was like a god, deciding the fates of neighborhoods and people. "From here, Colonia Lenin, you can get fine views. From the south, you can realize why Havana harbor was so important, protected from the sea."

I pointed out to some structures sticking out of a nineteenth-century neighborhood.

"A day care center. And an ugly Lenin statue. Built in 1911. First place to mark Lenin outside the Soviet Union. In the 1970s, there were some new buildings. . . . They were bad, unsustainable. Leaking was incorporated in these buildings from the beginning. Joints leak."

But buildings were not just buildings, and Mario Coyula wasn't just an architect and an urban planner. The structures were embodiments of ideas.

"The major problem with the Revolution is that it offered everything to the people, and they hadn't much in their pocket. It was hard to sustain all the advances we made in health care, education, et cetera, and to expand competitiveness. . . . For the city, we need to preserve buildings by increasing income. . . . The government owns about eighty-five percent of the housing. In 1960 there was the urban reform law, and rent wasn't paid anymore. This contributed to inflation. A vicious circle of disrepair. People didn't fix houses. If you had money, there was nothing you could do with it. It wasn't a matter of making people affluent if they couldn't go across the street and buy anything with it. . . ."

"What can you do now?"

"In my opinion, even if private construction was not encouraged, looked at with suspicion, two-thirds of housing repair was done through private money. We must encourage low-interest loans. Use locally made building materials. Rent equipment from the state."

The laser light danced over the city. "We are trying to push a metropolitan park along the river, to the mouth of the river. We are working on this project with students from Virginia Tech in Georgia. The park will follow the Malecón this way, along Fifth Avenue west. . . . Eliminate that shantytown over there. . . . Eliminate this shipyard. Here, we could create a large real estate zone. Have public space in front. Works as an equalizer for nature. We must restore the ecology. . . ."

Mario smiled quickly. "For many years, Cuban society was egalitarian."

I got it. This was a bittersweet joke: Cuban society had been egalitarian, but nature had been left out of this equality. Now it was time to restore nature, along with other more or less equal forces, such as enterprise, private initiative, self-interest. I was pleased, too, that American university students were involved with this project.

"We had a competition for the redesign of Central Havana," Mario said. "Many good drawings came out of it. But where the money will come from . . . ."

The laser danced. "Here is something I don't like. Mansions in the Vedado are being changed into dollar stores. Big old stores are being changed into homes. You're dealing with all sorts of sewer problems. The Cuban market is a captive market. . . . Oh, look, someone stole the church from this corner here."

The hall was occasionally open to the public. Mario was upset.

"When did you build your first building?" I asked, to get his mind off the theft of the church.

"In 1957. One building."

"Your career must span the entire noncultural period."

"Well, I was a student opposing Batista when the Revolution came. I was in the artistic vanguard."

"There was a vanguard in Russia too, until Stalin."

"It was different in Cuba. My group attacked Batista. Many of us were killed. Years later, I designed a monument for all the students who fought. I didn't protest very much the noncultural period. We were in power . . . well, maybe . . . maybe we are in power."

That was unexpected. Mario had looked back wistfully and, I thought, with some regret, on his own mistakes in the service of the regime. At the same time, he had questioned, spontaneously, whether he (and, doubtless, his intellectual friends) had power in Cuba. It was a perversely satisfying glimpse at a creature of a particular history. His reformist Romanian counterparts had been likewise caught between the ideals of their youth, an embarrassing Stalinist past, and now, an emerging capitalism. It could not have been morally satisfying.

But I also knew that if Cuba somehow managed this third way (though I doubted it), Mario Coyula would survive the storm of political change and surface with even more power in a post-communist government. First, because he was a passionate intellectual and professional who knew all the details of his domain, and second, because he knew the fine art of compromise and meaningful ambiguity.

We asked Mario to join us for lunch, but he had an appointment. He looked through his pockets and found the business card of his favorite restaurant: "La Cocina de Lillian Paladar (limited to 12 seats) Calle 48 #1311."

Mario Coyula

LILLIAN'S PALADAR

Set back in a garden behind a pleasant Spanish villa, Lillian's was a gracious oasis of good taste. The few tables were set in the shade beneath flowering arbors, next to a small fish pond, flanked by discreet statues of marble fauns and nymphs. There were tablecloths, fine silverware, and delicate antique porcelain plates. The elegant and handsome Lillian showed us to the table herself, and recommended a Spanish wine. A dessert cook was flaming brandy over some sweet confections at a table set against the adobe wall of the house. Everything about Lillian's cried: Forget the outside world! Don't think about misery, the masses, the *Barbudo,* or the embargo.

"So far," David pronounced with a hint of hope, "this Cuban food ain't been so hot." He was right, literally and figuratively. I'd thought that Cuba being tropical, Cuban food would be spicy, but so far we'd been treated only to blandness. Yellow rice, unseasoned black beans, mild chicken stews, fried pork chops, mashed potatoes, fruit, and rice with reconstituted milk. I hadn't even seen a bottle of hot sauce, which made me think longingly of New Orleans and my collection of hot sauces from Tabasco to habanero. Now, *habanero* means "from Havana," and habanero peppers were, as far as I knew, the hottest peppers anywhere, so it didn't make much sense that these tropical folks ate like Spaniards with ulcers.

"The food is spicier in Santiago and Trinidad," explained Ariel.

The handsomely printed menu at Lillian's listed three cream soups, a lamb stew, two chicken dishes, pork chops and yams, a cauliflower stew, three different fish dishes, two vegetarian ratatouilles, and several fine desserts. The basic materials were no different from those used in other *paladares* where we'd fed, but there was delicate care here and a sense of elegance resolutely missing elsewhere. It reminded me of a remark someone had made about a French artist during the war: "He ate roots, but what roots! He cooked them superbly!" I ordered the mushroom soup, fish, and ratatouille, and lay back, sipping the wine, suffused with the pleasure of the mild afternoon and that of my company.

Ariel recounted what she'd eaten in her guerrilla days. "The FMLN cuisine was mostly beans and tortillas. The women made tortillas in a trench so the fire wouldn't be seen. Now and then we caught a goat and, on a good day, we hijacked a truck full of eggs and had omelettes for a month."

"Not bad," said Art, who is a vegetarian. "That's probably better food than Cubans eat now."

"Sure, but do you see any fat Cubans?" said David. "This Fidel diet is pretty good for the figure." He patted his belly. "I could use some trimming."

I remembered that in the late 1980s and mid-1990s, when Romanians were starving, the dictator had gone on television and told people that not eating was healthy. I think this, more than anything else, sealed his fate.

The mushroom soup was unbelievable. There were three kinds of fresh mushrooms in it, a touch of coriander, and sherry. Its divine vapor made me weep. I looked around in a daze at all the other diners—the restaurant was full—and I thought I saw transported faces. I saw also that the well-dressed customers bore more than a passing resemblance to Mario Coyula—not physically, but spiritually. This was a *nomenklatura* restaurant, a place for the higher echelons. The better brass was definitely fed up with Castroism if they preferred a private restaurant that served no beef to a state restaurant that had everything plus bad service. Yes, the times they were a-changing.

After lunch we strolled through the house, which had been restored by the Spanish husband of the Cuban proprietor. It had a cool tiled patio, handwoven quilts on the wall, big ceramic jars on the floor. There were framed dried flowers, an old colonial art form dating back to the European discovery of new plant species on the island. There was an old sewing machine, an antique telephone, and music boxes on top of dark walnut dressers. The hallway had a gallery of daguerreotyped ancestors. A big fluffy dog was asleep under an elegant table with handmade lace covering it. The entire house, like the garden, was a delicate but emphatic protest against the proletariat.

ZOILA LAPIQUE

Zoila Lapique, sixty-seven, professor of history at Havana University, had a cold. The lovely living room of her 1920s Spanish-style villa was dark and cool. I made out some Botero-like paintings of large, stylized women on the walls. Small sculptures sat on top of bookcases and on a center table.

"My grandfather's work," said Professor Lapique, suggesting with that single phrase an artistic and intellectual pedigree that went back.

Just how far back, I found out after she invited us into her crowded study off the main hall. A splendid old cat stretched on top of a stack of documents on her desk.

"My ancestors," she said, her voice cracking, "settled in Louisiana before they came to Cuba. I have always been interested in New Orleans. I was very glad when you called. I would like to connect with a university researcher who could help me trace my family."

New Orleans and Havana were both modeled after the Spanish city of Cádiz—only on a different scale. Old Havana was both grander and much bigger than the French Quarter. Still, both cities had stuccoed buildings, wrought-iron balconies, courtyards with lush blooms, and mezzanines with high ceilings. The kinship between the two cities was the reason for our visit to Zoila Lapique, architectural historian. But it was clear now that, perching before us amid a jumble of books and manuscripts, was a passionate and outspoken scholar for whom history was anything but impersonal. This was true of others on this history-mauled island, but Zoila lived in it viscerally. She was already elaborating the connections between our cities, citing documents, searching for papers under her chair, and fighting her severely strained voice. I reached into my bag for some medicines. I handed her a bottle of aspirin and a box of cold capsules, which she thanked me for and ripped open without interrupting her train of thought. She swallowed two of each without water, and said: "If you look at the Havana coat of arms, you will see a key. The port of Havana was key to the European conquest of the Americas and to the expansion of trade from west to east."

"Professor Lapique," I said, "we would like to ask you about contemporary Havana."

She continued without hearing me. We were treated to a complete history of the port of Havana from its earliest days until the nineteenth century. A Zoila look-alike came in with a glass of water. "My sister," Zoila said. "I have no idea what I'd do without her. Our crucial position allowed Cuba to develop more rapidly than other nations in the area and our relations to the United States have always been important."

"Havana," I reminded her. "It is clear that the city is in an advanced state of decay. What will it take to reverse this?"

Finally, she heard me.

"Sadly, the process of deterioration is quite advanced. The owners abandoned the old houses, so they became *solares*, where people divided them up. They invested very little money to make them better. When the triumph of the Revolution came, these people in the *solares* were living in very bad conditions. They damaged their buildings to get out of that life, hoping that the Revolution would give them new houses. In the euphoria of the moment, they thought they were going to move. Many of these people were very poor and careless. No one was interested in city culture. Many people were inept. There weren't any resources."

Ariel struggled to translate Zoila's speech-*fleuve*, even as the historian kept talking right over the translation. But in the interstices, I had a little time to reflect. The stock phrase "the triumph of the Revolution" gave away Zoila's strong attachment to the status quo. Most people just said "the Revolution," leaving "the triumph" out of it. I had already gathered, from her determined manner and something indefinable in her person, that Zoila was a Revolutionary loyalist. There is a certain style I have come to know instinctively over the years as classically communist. I like it despite what I know it stands for. There is a kind of intelligent, passionate, opinionated stubbornness in old communists that keeps them young. And with the statements "No one was interested in city culture" and "Many people were inept," Zoila had criticized the government. The "inept" people were not the same people who "damaged" their homes. I decided to push it.

"What about the Soviet-style buildings? Who moved in there?"

"When I said 'inept,' I said it with the conviction of my sixty-seven years. There are some functionaries who are incapable of defending the city. I don't like Central Havana. You feel like you are walking through a city that's been bombed. In Central Havana you see eclectic-period buildings. But the city there is an architectural disaster. The city has been in the hands of people with no understanding of it."

Pretty strong words for a loyalist.

"What's going to save it?" I asked again.

"The strong arm of Eusebio Leal."

There again was the name of Eusebio Leal. It seemed that a good many young(ish) reformers bent on reestablishing the greatness of the city and renewing contact with the outside world were counting on him. Leal was part of an elite within the upper levels of power that was preparing Cuba for her postsocialist future.

I suggested that Cuba might be tired of strong arms. Zoila looked at me sternly and said: "The law is already breaking down. Old people are afraid in their own homes. A man came here one day because he saw one of my grandfather's sculptures through the window. He offered me fifty dollars for it, but I refused. He came back the next day and just took it and walked away. More and more old people are being killed in their homes for their antiques. What can I do? We are two old women here."

I could see how she might equate law and order with a strong arm. The underpaid police in Cuba were already exhibiting the symptoms of post-communism. In Romania, crime shot up after the end of the dictatorship. I hoped, for her sake, that Castro didn't unleash a Chinese-style "cultural revolution" in Cuba, where killing old people for their antiques would become a revolutionary requirement. The era of strong arms was over in most of the world, and the increase in crime that followed greater individual rights was part of the price. Better the greed crimes of capitalism than the mass crimes of ideology! But I let it pass: we were speaking across a gulf.

It was obvious that the city of Havana was Zoila's great love, but she said, "I am against habanocentrism," and then explained that the immigrants from the eastern provinces to Havana have overtaxed the city. "It makes sense to improve other cities, to stem the migration."

I wasn't sure whether the formula "against habanocentrism" was Zoila's own, or whether it belonged to the new Gorbachevist language of the reformers. The formula sounded hip, in a kind of American way, but it may have reflected a new Party policy. Or an old Party policy. I'd

Zoila Lapique

gotten the impression, from Zoila herself and from Mario Coyulo, that the city of Havana was very much at the center of the reformist plan for Cuba.

We parted affectionately. I had enjoyed Professor Lapique's lectures and her willful disregard of her cold. While David took some pictures, Ariel patted the cat and Zoila launched into a lecture about the venerable animal—a complete biography of the feline, really. I admired the artworks in the chiaroscuro of the living room. The shades were partly drawn, for fear of thieves.

Zoila waved good-bye as we pulled out in our vintage Oldsmobile, and I felt quite irrationally that I was saying good-bye to a friend. The mysteries of sympathy are great and, quite often, have nothing to do with philosophical differences. "I really liked her," I said.

"Me, too," agreed Ariel.

Art and David nodded, too. Well, there it was, the whole prickly team charmed by an old commie.

LOHANIA ARUCA

exquisite corpse no. 7

Karl Marx is a shit but we
are beyond that in the oldest
cemetery in the New World
& Cuba with bearded symbols
and long hair requesting
to be touched during a gathering
of poets in Havana—
Te espero sin odio;
con pena; con amor!
Tears of love and loss,
a slowness revealed in
flowers with rigid petals
grown in flesh fresh
earth-bound angels
drinking Castro's golden piss;
you're in it deep, deep, deeper;
shit shoveled
pero sentiendo la eternidad
de la vida—no vida
La dolce vida, very good,
yet semi-sweet
kisses the dead good-bye
& brings the absent landlords
back to the gates of their
own tombs in the cemetery

—Andrei Codrescu, David Graham, Art Silverman, Ariel Pena, and Lohania Aruca* (written December 12, 1997, in Cristóbal Colón Cemetery)

---

*I have to admit, to my eternal shame, that I set poor Lohania Aruca up in this corpse. After I explained to her the rules of our collaboration, she sweetly agreed to participate. I knew that she was a dedicated Communist, so I wrote "Karl Marx is a shit . . . ," folded the paper, and passed it on to her. Trustingly, she forged on. I didn't feel guilty but I did have a twinge of terror at the end, when she said, "Let's see what we all wrote." "That's impossible," I said, "we cannot look at our poems until the end of our visit. But . . . I'll send you a copy." I'm a wretched human being.

Professor Lohania Aruca, former director of the Cristóbal Colón Cemetery, treated us to orangeades and rum. She thrust a thick book of photographs of the cemetery into my hands and disappeared into the bathroom of her small, modern apartment to put on her makeup. She had an appointment with a Dutch television crew later that morning. The professor had written the text accompanying the photographs, but before I could read any of it, she reappeared, looking pretty much the same. She was ready to show us what she called, lovingly, "the fourth most important cemetery in the world."

The streets around the Cristóbal Colón were jammed because, I was surprised to find out, it was Havana's only cemetery and was very much in use. Four funerals were going on simultaneously, with gangs of mourners following behind hearses, trying not to follow the wrong one. It was hard to see how they kept it straight. Doubtless, many of these people were going to end up at the wrong funeral. We dashed across the boulevard and paused before the imposing gate to the necropolis. Professor Aruca stopped dead center before it, causing several streams of grieving *habaneros* to part. Pointing to the top of the arch, she drew our attention to details. There were inverted torches, symbols of death; branches of myrtle tied with ribbons, symbols of resurrection; and a child, representing a soul newly arrived in heaven, as well as a profusion of other symbolic figures, over the inscription "Janua Sum Pacis" (I am the doorway to peace).[35] There wasn't anything Cuban about this byzantine-romanesque monument, but it was impressive.

There was some very Cuban confusion about the visitors' fee at the entrance, though, because former cemetery director Aruca, after warmly hugging the girl at the ticket counter, had given us to understand that, being her guests, we didn't have to pay. This was, of course, an entirely unreasonable assumption on my part, based on capitalist museum directors I had known. Cuba needed dollars, the cemetery needed dollars, and the director could do only so much. We had but penetrated the stately boulevard of death that stretched, flanked by great monuments, to a domed chapel in the distance, when the ticket girl caught up with us, demanding dollars. This unnerved David, who was in the process of snapping a noble sugar merchant's tomb, but didn't faze the professor, who continued lecturing intensely on the ages of the cemetery and its grand architecture. I paid the gatekeeper, without taking my eyes off Lohania. Like Zoila and Mario, she was passionate about her subject, to the exclusion of most earthly matters. David huffed, annoyed at the slow pace of the proceedings. He and I had plans to go that afternoon to the Malecón to photograph and interview the conga line of miniskirted *jineteras* hitchhiking. I could see how that appointment could claim some priority over the extraordinarily detailed description of funerary art by the world's foremost expert on Cuban graves. We were shallow Yankees. In describing her cemetery, the professor was speaking about much more, of course. There was no subject in Cuba that did not jump at some point into history and politics.

"The cemetery is organized like a city. And it has a structure, a class structure. In this side of the cemetery, there is the zone of monuments of the first category. Wealthy industrialists, politicians, generals. So, in this zone, you will find historical characters, individuals who are very important to Cuba."

"In Romania," I said, "I used to go to the cemetery to think. There was no room in my house."

If Lohania made the connection she gave no sign. But it was true. In crowded countries, cemeteries are great for escape. I had also first made love in a cemetery. A Polish artist who'd led a high school strike had taken his classmates to the Warsaw cemetery to study "the real history," not the lies they were taught in school.

We inched past grand mausoleums of Revolutionary heroes interred beneath bombastic verses, forgotten generals weighed down by purple tributes, captains of industry in architect-designed houses, sugar barons in royal tombs, heavily eulogized writers and artists. Had I been more familiar with Cuban novels and romances, I'd doubtless have recognized the characters of their dramas. Professor Aruca could easily have spent a day with each tomb, but she remembered her appointment with Dutch TV and picked up the pace a bit. Still, she was visibly annoyed by Art's suggestion that she show us "the three most important graves in the cemetery."

"Three?" she snapped. "What is it with Americans? The bottom line? The best of? The ten best-dressed people? You are very impatient."

We came to a relatively modern monument. A white, art-nouveauish angel held a flowing body in her arms. The figures floated out of a black marble background. This striking sculpture, called *Piedad* (Pity) adorned an empty tomb. Noticing a birthdate chiseled in the marble, but no death date, I asked: "When was this tomb built? What period?"

"In 1959, was the end the tomb."

"So the family fled Cuba, and the tomb is unoccupied?"

"Unoccupied."

"I don't understand. What happens if they come back dead? Do they get buried here?"

"If they leave the property in Cuba with some family or some friends, they have the right to be buried here. It's no problem, because there are many people in the United States who send their family to the cemetery of Havana. But you have to have the property in advance."

"I see. So it would be a shame if they came without any papers and just hung around in front of their own tomb."

"You leave the property, then you leave everything. You see? One thing I reflect on many times is, how rich could be a person that can leave everything? It's just fantastic. You have to be very sure of yourself and your life and everything to leave everything."

"I certainly left everything in Romania when I was nineteen years old. We couldn't take anything with us. Not even the photographs that my mother took, because she was a photographer and we couldn't take that. I couldn't take the early poetry that I wrote. It was everything. So it was really a very painful process of being born again."

"Anyway, I don't think I wouldn't fight for something I love. When the Revolution came, I said, 'I will give my life to this country.' I have given my life to my country, my people. It's very difficult for me to understand. I know those on the other side, I know they may not understand me."

The bitter truth of Cuba was quite plain here before the empty tomb of the Aguilera family. Cuba was like a heart torn in two, an image carved on many of the funerary bas-reliefs around us. People had left their homes and gone into exile, but their dwellings had stayed behind to be inhabited by another generation, many of whom had also left in second and third waves of emigration. But the idea that the bodies of the Aguileras could arrive here at their burial place and be refused entry was even more awesome and absurd. They had fled alive but could not return even dead. There was no *piedad* here, history'd had no pity on anyone. I thought of Coyula's model of Havana—a world of buildings through which humanity washed in and out like the sea, its waves lifted by history.

What Lohania Aruca had just told me was complex. On the one hand, she'd let me know that she was patriotic, a supporter of the Party and Fidel, who would never think of abandoning the Revolution or Cuba. On the other hand, she had put the question in purely material terms. Professor Aruca, unlike Mario and Zoila, had not assumed automatically that we were friendly Yankees, already sold on Castroism, like most Americans who visited the island. Professor Aruca had sensed, quite correctly, that our group had two poles, an antistatist Eastern European and an all-American boy (David), who had to have things put to them in the simplest terms. Art, she had probably thought, was more sympathetic, and she must have trusted Ariel implicitly. Of course, David paid no attention at all to her profession of faith before the Aguileras' empty grave, while Art was professionally sympathetic and privately a classic liberal and no friend of Castro's. Only Ariel, the former *ideológico* and guerrilla fighter, would have been Professor Aruca's match in a real debate. But this was no real debate, and we merely skimmed the surface of the vast necropolis built around the missing body of the white discoverer of the Americas. We flitted, like bats, and the girls on the Malecón beckoned. On the other side of this seawall, ninety miles and a world away, was the whole other Cuba of the Aguileras, waiting to get back into their old homes and graves.

Lohania Aruca

The weather had turned. A drizzly rain was falling and the wind was banging the street signs and driving the sea over the Malecón. A couple of goose-bumpy *jineteras* waited under their umbrellas for a ride, but cars didn't stop. David put away his cameras.

On the way back to the hotel, two willowy teenagers attached themselves to us. "My whole life," one of them said, "I want to see the show at the Copacabana. If I save all my salary at the factory for a year, I could go." The other one added: "Yes, she could go, but she couldn't also buy a Coca."

"How sad." I felt for them.

"If you fall for that, you're a real chump," mumbled David.

"I never saw the show, either," said Art.

The Copacabana, formerly the Hilton, had turned its most cavernous meeting room into a show extravaganza. The place was jammed with Cuban women on the prowl for tourists. Gaggles of balding German men in shorts were drinking beer with two girls on their lap. Every nationality of middle-aged man was smothered in café-au-lait bounty at low tables laden with drinks.

"Like pigs in shit," quoth David.

Our own escorts, once seated and set up with Coca, became utterly fascinated by the show. The theme seemed to be fashion. Row on row of extravagantly costumed dancers under the operatic direction of a sadist with a whip shimmied unto the floodlit stage. They danced to various disco sounds with chorus-line precision. Our teenagers had totally forgotten us, absorbed by the stage. After each performance, a DJ called on the patrons to dance. Art, who liked to dance, took our new friends to the floor. The Cuban girls flowed more than danced and it was painfully obvious that Art, like all the other white males in the room, was being painfully outboogied. At some point, the girls abandoned him and came back to the table to drink more Coca. When Art had extricated himself from the sticky mass, he went to the bar to get some mineral water. A sophisticated and elegant beauty, sipping a Chivas Regal from a crystal tumbler, asked him: "What do you like to do?" "Dance," Art replied. "Dance, dance, dance!" "And do you," the beauty said, "also like to fuck, fuck, fuck?" Art beat a hasty retreat to our table, told his story, and said his good-byes.

"He doesn't like us?" one of the teenagers asked.

"Very much, but it's past his bedtime."

"We are good in school, we really are."

"When we go."

"What do you study?"

"Economics, of course."

We laughed over that one. They'd picked the wrong investment tonight, though. I said good night.

DAY FIVE: "THE PROLETARIAT WAS THOROUGHLY EROTICIZED"

exquisite corpse no. 8

The proletariat was thoroughly eroticized
when the dictatorship of the proletariat
collapsed
& the salt was not necessary
Black & white, colored
fish and a side of Che
"Bolus," she crowed,
removing her torso, but not
the perfect shape of womanhood
putting the tree into perspective
I thought that the thing
he was holding *era lo que yo*
deseaba en ese momento
Black & white octopus and girl
now we see where she's put the crab
and we crush the lobster
White people are ugly they no
do the octopus dance

—**Ariel Pena, Andrei Codrescu, David Graham, and Art Silverman**

THE BEACH

The astute reader will have deduced from the above corpse two essential things about the fateful day of December 13, A.D. 1997, namely that we were at the beach while writing it, and that we had reached that stage in our gang life when we became *eroticized!* But before we get to this all-important outing and exceedingly precarious state, allow me to recount the day in proper order.

Art, David, and I met over the buffet. I examined groggily the sprinkling of film fest Europeans and noticed Al Lewis having a zesty breakfast of everything and holding forth to a family of starstruck Latin Americans. Eventually, my ear drifted to a couple at a neighboring table.

"I heard," the woman said in English with a Spanish accent, "that an entourage of two thousand is coming with John Paul II to Cuba. And they are bringing two Popemobiles."

"I heard," said the man, "that the Pope is renting the Rolling Stones' sound system."

The strains of "Sympathy for the Devil" wafted through my head. Now, wouldn't that be something? One million people in Plaza de la Revolución, site of Fidel's greatest speeches, the place yellow with papal banners, and the Rolling Stones' sound system booming the Rolling Stones' greatest hits? Sorry. In the morning the fancies of dreaming still cling to me. But whether the Pope used the Stones' amps or not, the crowds were expected to exceed Fidel's biggest. Rumor had it that, fearing this, the government was providing no public transportation for the papal visit, and that the buses donated to the Church from abroad were inadequate. Most people were expected to make their way on foot from small towns and villages as well as distant neighborhoods of Havana.

We needed a break from the masses. Arturo was happy to take us to the beach.

Arturo happy to take us to the beach

The beaches of Cuba were famous enough to be noted by all the early travel writers. In the 1960s, they became notorious locales for illicit, especially homosexual, sex.

Which beach was best suited for us was a subject of some debate between Arturo and other well-meaning folk who overheard us pondering. In Cuba, all conversation becomes a matter of public interest if anyone overhears you. A gentleman with a toothpick opined that the "tourist beaches" built recently by Spanish, Italian, and Cuban joint ventures, were of no interest to anyone "but tourists." "On a real Cuban beach," he said, "you can see the passion." Since we were obviously tourists, he concluded, "Go where you can spend the money. Don't listen to me." A young, scholarly man with square ebony glasses whispered, "Cuba is an island. Most of our beaches are targets for the CIA. You should go swim at Playa Girón." There was a thought. Go for a dip in the Bay of Pigs.

"That's one way to look at it," I said. "Another is that every Cuban beach is a way out of Cuba. There is the beach at Mariel, for instance."

The young man laughed, but our driver wasn't pleased. Arturo, whose 1956 Dodge we'd been tootling along in, had become our full-time driver because we liked him, though his mustache spelled "police" to me. He claimed to speak no English, but he laughed at our jokes in English. This, by the way, is the best way to flush out a spy who claims not to speak your language: make a really stupid joke and watch him laugh. That's how I cracked my Securitate driver in Romania, a boyish-looking man who turned out to speak not only English but also German, Russian, and French. His English, he claimed when he couldn't hide anymore, was from television. He loved *Dallas.*

Arturo steered us into his cab and said, "The Cuban beach is very crowded. Young people make trouble all the time. Tourist beach is nice, clean, no trouble."

That settled it. We were going to the Cuban beach. I have always prized the people's beaches over all others. On Chesapeake Bay in Maryland, I had particularly enjoyed a stretch of sand called "the tattoo-and-hickey beach," where every bather sported one or the other or both. Since then, I have found that every shoreline has its tattoo-and-hickey beach, pulsing defiantly amid the forces of progress.

The people's beach was a ribbon of sugary sand squiggling at the edge of the azure Caribbean. The air was crisp and brilliant. The water was transparent; you could see fish and sand on the bottom. The coral

reef was penciled in the distance like a thin, dark mustache. A catama-
ran with a crudely lettered sign, "For Hire," bobbed a few feet out on
the water. A man sleeping near it waved unenthusiastically. Later, he
came over and offered to take us to the reef. We told him to come back
later, but he never did.

A few boys were standing around a brilliant electric-blue fish, a lobster, and an enormous squid that had just been pulled out by one of
them. I walked past them into the water, a lukewarm salt bath, and
floated on my back. The gentle waves carried me out. There were a few
wispy clouds in the brilliant blue, spelling out a loose approximation of
the letters O and K. I found it hard to believe that this gentle water was
licking the shore of embattled Cuba. If I allowed myself to be taken by
the waves, I might end up anywhere in the Caribbean.

I returned to the towel I'd spread in the sand. Ariel sat a distance
away under a tree, writing in her notebook. Art and David had gone for
a walk on the beach. I watched women in the merest of bikinis walk by,
rolling their hips as if they were dancing, and muscular boys and men
in tight nylon bikinis that left nothing to the imagination. One of them,
a dark, muscled young man with an evil-looking patch over his right
eye, plopped next to me on the sand. He readjusted leisurely his manly
endowment, and asked: "Anything you like? Cigar? Pussy? Taxi?"

After I said no, he told me that his name was Manuel, that he'd
been part of the Cuban Olympic team in Munich in 1972, that he'd
fought in Angola, and that he was training again now for a shot at professional welterweight boxing. He was a lot older than I'd thought, and
judging by the dragon tattoo on his left arm, he may also have done a
stint in jail between the Olympics and Angola. Or after. As he talked,
my eye wandered to two Afro-Cuban bodies marching in G-strings
down the sand.

"You want them?"

"No, thanks"—pointing to Ariel reading innocently under the
tree—"my girlfriend."

"No problem." Manuel winked, "You come do it right in the
water . . . boom, boom. Want I talk to them? Your girlfriend don't see
nothing."

That was actually funny, but laughing didn't endear me to Manuel,
who projected an air of menace beneath his hustle. He kept eyeing
David's cameras and Art's bag as well, so I was loath to leave, though I
really felt like going for a swim again.

"Sorry, Manuel, but not today."

Finding himself at the bottom of his *jinetero* bag, he asked bluntly: "Want to fuck me? Suck my cock?"

I declined politely, but when he didn't go away I gave him two dollars. He left grumbling, his huge fists closing for a moment, bad vibes steaming off him. I was quite convinced that if we'd been alone in a more isolated place, he would have harmed me. This was the first time I'd encountered any real hostility in Cuba.

When David and Art came back, we sat at the small beach restaurant and ate the blue fish while a beautiful woman posed for two men with the huge octopus, leaning against a tree. Two other thong-bikinied beach bum-ettes were swaying to the salsa music coming from a portable radio. Blue skies, swaying palms, sugar-fine sand, perfect bodies, divine fish, la dolce vita . . . I was in suspended bliss.

While eating the blue fish, we were approached by a petite woman with a satchel full of jewelry, which she displayed on the table, blithely declaring: "I stole them from the factory. I sell for half." There were tortoiseshell bracelets, pendants and earrings of (illegal) black coral, mother-of-pearl Santería figures, silver-filigreed ivory boxes. We men looked through the glittery treasure, while Ariel and the jewel thief engaged in a political discussion. The jewel thief said that the Cuban people have three rights: "the right to free education, free medical care, and the right to steal from the state." Pablo's joke was ubiquitous. It reminded me of the saying in pre-1989 Romania: "They pretend to pay us, and we pretend to work."

The beach

Cuban joke number four. Or was it five?

A group of loud Italians arrived: the women watched the Cuban men on the beach with evident greed, while their spouses licked their lips and ejaculated loudly in the direction of the swaying *mulatas*. Paradise was, unfortunately, a meat market.

The beach

THE ANTIQUE PICTURE ALBUM

It was still early afternoon when we left the beach, so we asked Arturo to take us to Old Havana.

In the square of the cathedral in Old Havana, book vendors peddled the writings of Che and Fidel, but also complete sets of the works of Lenin, unopened and in pristine condition. At some point every petty bureaucrat on the island must have possessed a full shelf of the founding fathers. Lenin and Stalin were standard furniture for medium-level apparatchiks in Romania until the sheer mass of Ceaușescu's oeuvre displaced them. Che must have certainly been prolific: dozens of titles, from guerrilla war how-tos to heady assessments of industrial output, bore his name. Only Fidel's collected speeches and photo albums outweighed him. Among the *padres* of state communism only the founders had written more. Stalin had laid out the correct way to think in every science and branch of the humanities, in hundreds of volumes ghosted by collectives of Stalinists. Fidel had had no need of such collectives, because he'd found out everything he needed to know by speaking about it. His unbounded orality found its riverbed in six-hour bursts, which, transcribed, amounted to millions of words. Fidel was from the Ted Berrigan school of "I can't wait to hear what I'm going to say next"—which, at first, endeared him to his listeners because they, like him, were delighted by the surprises sure to follow; but then, when the surprises turned out to be made of a limited number of slogans, they fell into the deep sleep from which they haven't yet awakened. But, just in case, here were the books.

Che, on the other hand, had been a writer. His youthful works, like *The Motorcycle Diary,* were the record of the gradual hardening of his brain into ideological intransigence, charming because of the occasional glimpse into his beat/Hell's-Angel-in-Latin-America lifestyle of the 1950s. After he became an official of Revolutionary Cuba, his writings became conscious efforts at an oeuvre to rival the commie daddies. But at least they were writing. Che wrote a lot more than he spoke, and there is some speculation that he left Cuba not so much in order to spread revolution as to get away from Fidel's megamaniacal oratory.

The secondhand book dealers were not discriminating. After the stacks of unsold Ches and Fidels, which they must have acquired for a song from dollar-hungry apparatchiks at the ongoing remainder sale on socialist classics, they filled their shelves with all the other official product of the Cuban writerly class, in descending order of interest: the works of the state poet Nicolás Guillén, the novels of the Writers' Union–approved Alejo Carpentier, the scores of volumettes spewed under the auspices of the Casa de las Americas, historical and archival treatises approved by the historical and archival institutions, and so on. The salable items in ascending order were: photo albums of the Revolution, which were of great interest to German tourists, the later works of Hemingway, Cuba's second most famous bearded man, the novels of Gabriel García Márquez, Fidel's chief PR man in Europe, pre-Revolutionary illustrated magazines, and Spanish-English dictionaries.

I browsed with mild interest, obviously amused by the masses of unsold *jefe* works. When it became clear to one of the vendors that nothing in his visible piles was of burning interest to us, he winked and beckoned me behind the shelves.

"I'll show you something." From the bowels of a box under a canvas covering, he pulled several turn-of-the-century illustrated books. One of these caught my attention. It wasn't a printed book, but an album of small, hand-tinted photographs. They were photos of women, children, brides and grooms, and *filles-de-joie,* taken between 1890 and 1910. The vendor explained that each photo came inside a cigar box during those decades and that the album was the work of a diligent collector. It was, in fact, quite extraordinary. There were bosomy Victorian ladies with extravagant hats. Pinups of actresses posing to titillate the cigar smokers. Scores of Victorian children dolled up like small adults. Brides in the flush of bridedom. Costumed sylphs, harpists, and milkmaids. Couples dancing.

He wanted three hundred dollars for it, but after a bit of haggling that attracted several other book dealers, I got him down to a hundred and fifty. I was aware that such an object could be easily construed by the customs as contraband, so I asked for a receipt. He wrote out an elaborate receipt with the date and some kind of name—surely not his—and the album was mine. I still sensed trouble. I was right.

**Book stalls in
Havana Vieja**

STATE SECURITY

exquisite corpse no. 9

when the pig strikes
fight him with futile fury
to frustrate him with spaghetti
with humanity at arm's length
the straitjacket of Cuba
is made of little men
with little power—
it always comes
like a sharp scream
that everyone ignores
out of fear.

—Ariel Pena, Art Silverman, David Graham, and Andrei Codrescu

We returned to the Hotel Capri for an afternoon of rest, note-taking, and regrouping. Next day we were going to Santiago de Cuba, at the eastern end of the island. We made plans to meet Ariel in the early evening for dinner.

The sun had made me lightheaded and I had been feeling a distinct lack of gravity, as if the beach had somehow detached me from all serious preoccupations. I felt frivolous, and I wondered, all the way down to the lobby, what it would take to make me a serious person again. I saw Ariel waiting in the area near the elevators and waved when I saw her. One of the hotel security guards was approaching her from another direction. We reached her almost simultaneously.

"Ready for dinner?" I asked.

"You leave here now!" the guard hissed to Ariel.

"I am a translator for foreign journalists," she answered politely.

"If you don't leave now, you will be arrested."

"Why?"

I backed up a step. Official types bring my blood to a boil quickly. I can't even abide rudeness from bank tellers. "What is the problem?"

"She has to leave."

"Why?" Ariel asked again.

"Look, Comrade, Ms. Pena is working for us. If you don't like it, you can go on being nasty and end up dead meat when your boss finds out."

The guard spoke into his walkie-talkie and three similar police types with mustaches and guayabera shirts appeared, trailed in short order by the squat blond woman I'd seen in the lobby before. David and Art arrived at the same time.

Ariel asked once more what the problem was. The first guard jabbed her arm spitefully with his index finger and said, "You're dark-skinned!"

"So you think I'm a *jinetera* because I'm dark-skinned?" Ariel's voice rose slightly here, and I feared for the policeman. She could probably have killed him with one hand. Petite and pretty Ariel had been trained by the FMLN.

I took out my notebook and pen. Instinctively, Art took out a microphone and shoved it close to the policeman's mouth. He had already begun recording. The microphone was for show. David pointed a camera. The purpose of this journalistic assault was the thought that most petty officials are afraid of the media. In the United States, if you threaten to tape someone, they sometimes back off. Not in Cuba.

The four security guys lined up behind the blond woman, who said firmly: "Your passports, please!"

"Let me get this straight," I said, "You are ejecting our translator from the hotel because she is dark-skinned. And then you tell everyone that there is no racism in Cuba! And now you are taking our passports. Are we under arrest?"

Ariel translated this, which enraged the Cubans. They led us to the couches at the far end of the lobby. We handed over our passports. One of the men examined Ariel's passport and said: "Salvadorena?" Now, this was quite a thing to be, in the wake of the big fuss Cuba had made about the Salvadoran national who'd recently bombed tourist sites in Havana. On top of that, we were Americans, the official enemy. It occurred to me, too, that as Americans we had no representation. The U.S. interest section in Havana is housed inside the Swiss embassy, and is not exactly equipped to save the asses of Americanos stupid enough to go to Cuba against their government's advice.

"You come with us," the blond woman said to Ariel. We rose to accompany her, but Ariel was calm. She said she'd handle it. She handed Art her cellular phone and told him to call her husband to explain the situation. Tom had been living in Havana long enough to know the ways of the natives. The policemen took Ariel through a door behind the registration desk.

Here we were, under house arrest in the lobby of our own hotel, without passports, and laden with incriminating notes, audiotapes, and photographs. We were painfully aware also that our visa was not for journalism. We were scholars, here for the Havana Film Festival. Art took his DAT tapes from his shoulder bag and started stuffing them, incongruously I thought, into his socks. I put my notebook under my belt. David did nothing, because he had too much film, but we discussed sending all our materials out of Cuba with a journalist, if we came out of this with the stuff still in our hands.

Art called Tom, who arrived quickly, speaking to officials in the Ministry of the Interior on his own cell phone. He didn't have much success, but he strode in through the door behind the lobby, despite the attempts of a desk clerk to stop him. He and Ariel were in there for over two hours. Meanwhile, a man with two stars on his shoulders, carrying a briefcase, walked by us in a hurry and disappeared through the same door.

After two hours, Tom and Ariel reappeared, accompanied by the blonde. Ariel was pale. I could only imagine how she felt. She had been detained by the fascist police in El Salvador, back when she thought that Cuba was socialist heaven, and now she had just experienced the socialist version. But Tom was calm: as a reporter for the BBC he had been questioned and detained several times.

The blonde pointed to the three of us and said: "Come!"

"We would like our translator," Art said.

The blonde pointed to me: "He's Romanian. He speak enough Spanish. I translate if I need."

The mysterious door led into a small windowless room. Seated before a metal desk was the starred official. Standing behind him were the hotel's policemen. The official was blunt:

"You are doing journalistic work in Cuba. You have no visa."

"No," I said, "we are here for the film festival. We are taking audio notes and photographs for a possible documentary on Cuba."

"You are Romanian. There were many Romanians here."

"Before."

"Before," he agreed.

"Can we listen to the tape you made in the lobby?"

"Sure," Art said. He listened to the tape on his DAT—ostensibly to cue it to the place—and erased in the process some of our incendiary interview with Pablo, our mulatto Virgil. (He had made a copy of it.) When he was done, he handed the tape to the blonde, who listened to it, but clearly did not understand very well.

"He says something about 'skin color,'" she said uncertainly.

"That's right," I said. "That man"—pointing to the security guard—"said that Ms. Pena's skin color was dark, so she couldn't be in the hotel. I thought that there was no racism in Cuba."

Of course, I had noticed plenty of it. While it was true that every day Cubans of every shade mixed quite freely and there was little of the hidden tension that attends race relations in the United States, there was plenty of discrimination. The poorest people, the inhabitants of Central Havana, were also the darkest. Castro's top brass was mostly white. While their country's own racism was hidden, the Cubans were quite open about discussing foreigners in ethnic terms. In Old Havana I encountered an Angola war veteran named Lenin González, a fierce patriot, now a *jinetero* by necessity, who told me that Africans were the laziest fighters he'd ever met. The Cubans had fought every battle, while the African soldiers and chiefs smoked kif and slept most of the time. Havana was full of Angola veterans—doctors, engineers, soldiers. The recent memory of Soviets and Eastern Europeans was a rich subject of conversation. The Russians seemed to have been universally disliked for their arrogance, high-handedness, refusal to speak Spanish, crass materialism. Poles were liked a lot better: they spoke Spanish, were Catholic, and had manners, passion, and so on. Even Romanians—mostly teachers and engineers—who'd been to Cuba had left behind a pleasant impression, though they had seemed frivolous even by Cuban standards.

My remark about skin color embarrassed the official. "No, it was not skin. He expressed himself wrongly. Cuban citizens are not allowed in tourist hotels for the protection of tourists. We don't want them to be bothered or maybe robbed. So far, how do you like the Hotel Capri?"

"Until this incident everything was fine."

"And how do you like Cuba?"

"Cuba is a beautiful country."

"Fine people," said David.

"Hospitable," added Art.

It was an exercise in futility. There was no clear reason to hold us. Higher officials might have been upset. The Interior Ministry cop asked each one of us in turn: "Are you going to do journalism in Cuba?"

We all said no, and they handed us back our passports.

I had the distinct feeling that we were going to be watched now. It was a good thing we were leaving Havana for Santiago next morning. Nobody knew about our plans, and surely the Havana office wouldn't alert the whole country about some possible journalists on the loose. After all, tens of thousands of journalists were set to descend on Havana in a few weeks for the Pope's visit. It wasn't smart to start out on the wrong foot. But just to be sure, that evening we gave all our tapes and notes to our PBS friend Pat Flynn, who was returning to the States the next day. Stoically, David refused to part with his film. "We go together, my film and I," he said, and I had a brief vision of him holding his film to his chest as the firing squad blindfolded him.

That night I kept my notes under the pillow and slept poorly, awakened by mustachioed men and questioned in my dreams. The blonde made a brief appearance, too, and I remembered that Ariel had whispered about her at some point: "In Cuba we call this type of women Soviet blondes. There used to be thousands of them when the Russians were here. They all work for the police."

The preacher next door was bringing another *jinetera* to Jesus, and his fervent prayers and laying on of hands mixed with the policemen in my dream to make an odd religious and atheistic collage, as if the Inquisition and the Cuban secret police were collaborating for my benefit. Of course, it all seemed quite natural, because I'm a Jew. I woke up with an odd smell in my nostrils, something I thought of as the universal smell of the police, an *eau de* boots, fear, sweat, and old uniforms. Plus a bit of priestly incense.

Our cellular phone, which had proved so useful the previous evening, died in the morning. We found the place in Miramar that would fix it. CEL-CUBA, Cuba's first cellular-phone company, was, naturally, a dollars-only business. A pretty policewoman in a short skirt was stationed solemnly in front of it. David took her picture and I talked with her. We flirted. Why not—I had dollars, socialism's chief good now. Her gun was very impressive, her smile very pretty. I asked her her name and she wrote it down: Yaslin Mayor Galvez. And then, smiling, she asked me to write down my name, my address, my telephone number, the hotel I was staying in, and my passport number. Quite a lot before I even asked her for a date.

Tom warned us to be careful leaving Cuba. Names of people suspected of funny business were usually passed on to the customs police, who could confiscate anything they found objectionable. Although we had sent off some of our materials with Pat, there was still plenty of contraband. The cigars we'd bought from Pablo, for instance. And the jewels from the self-professed thief at the beach. And the letters several Cubans had given to me to post in the United States because they didn't trust the Cuban mails. And, worst of all, the antique picture album.

DAY SIX

The need to be careful arose at the wrong time, because I had two covert operations in mind. I wanted to meet some Cuban writers, unofficial ones, and I wanted to meet some of the revolutionaries who lived in political exile in Havana.

Ariel had arranged a meeting with writers. The exiles were more difficult to find. I knew that some of them, including a few hundred Americans, had taken up permanent residence in the bosom of the mother ship when their insurrections had failed. The disappointed radicals floated like sunflower-seed husks along the Malecón, meeting in coffeehouses to discuss dashed hopes and the vanishing Revolution. Ariel knew the widow of Roque Dalton, the young Salvadoran poet who had been killed by his comrades in the early days of the war in El Salvador. I knew about William Lee Brent, a Black Panther who had been living in Havana since hi-jacking an airplane in Oakland in 1970. Brent had spent two years in a Cuban jail as a suspected spy. After his release, he'd worked in a meat plant, then gotten a college degree and ended up teaching English. He'd written a fascinating story called *Long Time Gone.*[36] There was also Joanne Chesimard, convicted of killing a cop in 1977; she had escaped from prison and had been living in Cuba for fourteen years. Her case got renewed attention in the United States when her defiant and unrepentant remarks were broadcast on television during the Pope's visit. Governor Christine Todd Whitman of New Jersey demanded her extradition.[37] There were other American fugitives, not all of them self-proclaimed revolutionaries, enjoying Castro's hospitality. There was former financier Robert Vesco, for instance, and Lorna Birdsall, who had been married to Manuel Pineiro, the now deceased former chief of the Cuban Intelligence Services. Interviewed recently and asked what she'd like people to bring her from America, she replied: "A Kmart."[38] These people interested me for several reasons. All revolutionaries have, at one time or another, clustered in a city of exile from where they proceeded concentrically to change the destinies of their countries. In the exile milieus, radicals, artists, con men, and adventurers mixed freely. Zurich, Switzerland, had been host before World War I to Lenin and his Russian revolutionaries. Paris had cuddled countless conspirators, from Trotsky to Pol Pot to the Ayatollah Khomeini. Mexico City in the 1950s had been the hub for Che

Guevara and Fidel Castro. In Mexico City, at that time, unbeknownst to the Latin revolutionaries, Jack Kerouac, William Burroughs, and Neal Cassady were bumming around, hatching their own revolution, an artistic one. In 1916, the Dadaist writers and artists in Zurich also rubbed shoulders with the Russian revolutionaries, with no idea of what the momentous future portended. I didn't think that Havana in late 1997 was home to any kind of ferment, either revolutionary or artistic, but the state of mind of exiles is always interesting and should never be ignored.

exquisite corpse no. 10

No words to say the secret names of salt
Point to me the guerrilla in the night's groin
The rum writes in sand
The names of our splendid socialist teeth
You can rattle the chain
but you can't touch the monkey!
Cards plastic, Harleys shiny.

—**Cuban writers, Ariel Pena, Art Silverman, Andrei Codrescu, and Tom Gibb**

We didn't find the exiles, but we met several unofficial writers who might as well have been exiles. Their detachment from the state-approved cultural institutions in Cuba was tantamount to exile.

We met the writers at the home of one of them. He lived with his mother, wife, and child in two rooms with a minuscule kitchen. Our host looked like Jim Morrison. The place was bourgeois by Cuban standards. Cuba, like Romania and every other socialist country, has a perpetual housing crisis. This is one of the many ironies of a system dedicated by definition to improving living conditions. For an economic system, socialism is strangely deficient economically. This problem almost transcends the philosophical opposition between capitalist liberalism and socialism; it's more like a curse. The problem, I think, is that when the Communists seized power they saw themselves as the providers of all good things to the deserving (i.e., the conforming) and in so doing they used up all the existing resources in record time, without being able to motivate people enough to create more. After all, if you're living in Paradise, why work? The Party will provide. The communist leaders were, of course, at pains to explain that no one was in Paradise *yet*. Socialism was not yet communism, and there were many painful stages to conquer. The current stage of misery in Cuba had been dubbed "La Lucha" (The Struggle) by Fidel, and all official stupidity and indifference, as well as plain mismanagement, were attributed to La Lucha, which became a kind of mystical dark star involving everyone in a war of some kind. Also ironically, Marxism, for all its rational pretensions, became a springboard for all kinds of mystical or plain occult beliefs in such things as Stages, Struggles, Five-Year Plans, Sugar Tonnage, Happiness, et cetera, et cetera. One can make a long dreary poem out of all the capitalized platitudes of these regimes. Most people—probably all people—in this type of society never believed the bad poetry of the state, but went along only for fear of the police. Or out of sheer laziness.

Anyway, here we were, in the bourgeois digs of a Cuban writer. His mother, a sweet lady, greeted us warmly, then retired somewhere in the back, leaving us to our own devices in a small room with two bottles of rum. The writers were a mixed group. Most of them wrote science fiction, a genre that was quite popular in Cuba. But their work, influenced by cyberpunk, a genre pioneered by the American William Gibson, was being published in Spanish and English outside the country.

I asked why science fiction was popular in Cuba.

"It allows us to speculate on the future with a degree of freedom not found in realistic fiction."

"Our generation," explained another, "is not interested in the current fashion for realistic fiction about the lumpen proletariat, the *jinetera* with the heart of gold, the soldier with the alcoholic mother, etc. We want to take part in the international conversation about culture."

The writers, in their late twenties and mid-thirties, were reacting to the new wave of approved stories concerned with the bitter social realities of Cuba. I understood them. Reality didn't have much cachet in the dying days of communism in Romania, either. The Eighties Generation, as Romanian writers of that era called themselves, disdained realism. They wrote fantastic tales for each other, using language play, musical techniques, vernacular, Western avant-garde collage and cut-up techniques. Similarly, the Cubans were resolutely ignoring the provincialism and isolation of their island.

"We act as if we are free," said one of them.

These writers were laying the basis for a post-communist civil society. To act "as if" one was free was to deny the state power over one's soul. Still, I had heard that Cuban writers were pretty free to experiment. They had never had an official doctrine such as "socialist realism" to dictate their subjects.

"That's somewhat true," the youngest writer there said. "You can write anything but for one thing. Him. In Cuba we say, 'You can rattle the chain, but you can't touch the monkey.'"

As the rum flew down our throats, literature and politics started to mingle with literary gossip and commentary on current schools of critical thought about writing in the United States. I was surprised at how well-informed the Cubans were. They had devoured every bit of literary news from abroad and had integrated it into their thinking. I felt almost nostalgic for their intellectual voracity. There was an intensity and seriousness in their concern for culture that were utterly lacking in the United States, where one is presented daily with a huge menu of choices. For these Cubans, culture wasn't a luxury, but food for creative survival.

We discussed Eastern Europe, and its meaning for Cuba. The collapse of socialism behind the Iron Curtain had been barely reported in the Cuban press. That brought us back to Him, the Hombre Invisible everything returned to and revolved around.

"It appears," one writer said, "that Napoleon, Fidel, and Clinton were talking. Napoleon tells Clinton, 'If I'd had your infantry I wouldn't have lost at Waterloo.' Then Fidel says, 'If you'd had *Granma,* nobody would have even heard of Waterloo.'"

The jokes were familiar to me. They came from the culture of the Joke, which was the common culture of all socialist countries. One can dispense with serious histories and study solely jokes for a complete picture of the birth, decay, and collapse of these regimes. The Stalin-era jokes, though quite innocent by late-Brezhnev standards, could have earned their tellers years at hard labor. Toward the end, the jokes were the only thing still holding the people together.

"We are so tired of the guy we never say his name."

"Yes. One man wrote on a wall: 'Down with You-Know-Who.'"

"And another started writing 'Down with . . .', then looked over his shoulder, didn't see any State Security, so wrote the letter 'F.' There was a tap on his shoulder and a secret policeman stood there. 'Excuse me,' the man said, 'I can't remember: Is it Flinton or Clinton?'"

We had a laugh over that one, not because it was particularly funny, but because it was so uselessly familiar. I told them that in Romania now the binding cement of political humor had all but crumbled, leaving in its wake the bitter taste of a hundred different specialized idioms. I told them also a little bit about the fate of writers in post-communism, a subject I knew they had little information about. Many dissident or faux-dissident scribblers had carved themselves political niches in the first post-communist governments, only to be quickly disillusioned by the turn of events. Bad economies and virulent nationalism had appealed to yet other writers (usually second- and third-raters who had flattered the communists), and they were rising stars of the rhetoric of hatred.

"Nationalism is now the order of the day in Cuba, too," one of them said.

"It always was," interjected another. "Castroism was never plain communism, it was mostly Castro and whatever he said was Cuban. That is the secret of his power."

That explained Castro's longevity. Never a simple ideologue, he had infused Cuban nationalism with his personality so that they were now inseparable. It made sense, then, that the consensus was that nothing would change in Cuba until Castro died. But then what? If Cuban nationalism was so full of Castro that the two could hardly be separated, then Castro's death would leave behind a dangerous force indeed, a force without direction that would defend itself blindly against whatever it perceived as a threat, whether Cuban exiles or the United States. But when I proposed this theory, one writer just laughed. "Cubans are too hungry to think about anything except food."

Not everyone agreed. As is often the case with rum-warmed writers, an argument ensued, one in which history, politics, literature, even French philosophers rushed in to help opinion. I realized that the transition of Cuba to whatever came next was not going to be easy. There was one opinion per person in the room. The only thing they had in common was that they were sick of the Maximum Leader. We all had rum in common, too, and when the bottles were empty, some of us went out to a jazz club. Rum and jazz were eternal, the rest was illusory.

The writers

DAY SEVEN: "ALMOST PERSIAN AT 15,000 METERS"

SANTIAGO DE CUBA

exquisite corpse no. 11

Almost Persian at 15,000 meters, she
sulks, clasped in a seatbelt trap
too husky to not bite so we bite
her mustache lit by soviet bulbs
planted in overhead steel
from Minsk, Novosibirsk, Amur,
pure ice but still her chiseled
Med flesh is smoking from beneath
the tight flower print skirt.
We rumble tonight toward the Oriente
de Cuba not yet fucked but fully
prepared; shielded from view
by a pale blue shower curtain
open to give head, cook spinach
and gyrate ravenous depleted eons
of travel, sprawled open-legged,
mumbling voodoo inside the fucking
Russian airplane getting sucked
into the Bermuda triangle, Cuban cube,
Haitian hexagon, *los paranoias,*
my *paladar* closes at dusk, adjust
her chastity belt for the big meeting
with Virgen's finger-fucked on a Castro
convertible, Fidel-ity Trust!

**—Art Silverman and Andrei Codrescu
(aboard a Russian plane to Santiago de Cuba)**

At the José Martí Airport, waiting for transport to the Oriente, David looked around at the huddled masses lugging huge parcels, crying, weeping, laughing, smoking, listening to small radios, and flirting, and asked: "What's happening here?"

I said: "Oh, just the usual mix of horniness and confusion."

This is the usual mix for all official Cuban offices open to the public: uncertain bureaucrats, confused mobs, flirting, no sense of line, lots of joyous nonsense, and an unmistakable sexuality.

On the bus taking us from the gate to the airplane, David pointed out a classic Spanish beauty with strong Mediterranean brows, an aquiline nose, and a bead of olive oil in the soft down of a nearly invisible mustache over her bright-red-lipsticked mouth.

On the plane, she sat next to a broom-brush mustachioed *hombre* in a suit who was reading *Granma*. She sneaked a sideways glance at him and arranged herself demurely in her seat, but her slit dress was open, revealing a healthy swatch of thigh. A few moments after takeoff, he showed her his ticket and asked something that made her laugh. She leaned closer to look at the ticket in his hand. After some study, she shrugged and laughed again. The man returned to *Granma*, but as we gained some altitude—it was hard to say how much, because we were in a windowless Soviet transport plane that made a sound like a bad truck—he put an arm around her shoulder, pulled her to him, and attempted to kiss her. He also laid a hand right in the slit of her summer dress, high on her bare thigh. She made a symbolic effort at removing the hand. Rebuffed by the symbolic effort (or maybe let off the hook by it), he let go and regained *Granma*. The economic figures must have meant the world to him, because he became completely absorbed.

All this had taken place in less time than it took me to write it. Left without his attention, the woman readjusted herself modestly. A while later she leaned ever so slightly toward the serious man. Things were quiet for a time; then, without warning, his hand landed again at the top of the slit of her dress and pushed its way between her tightly crossed legs. This time she let him, and leaned closer as if trying to look at his newspaper. A carnal effluvium wafted over our whole section of the plane like the year 1968.

The proletariat had been eroticized, all right. But then, weirdly, the *hombre* withdrew and returned to *Granma*! What had happened? The abandoned molestee regarded him angrily, then drew away from him and put on her seat belt ostentatiously—like a chastity belt. It was the first time I'd seen an airplane seat belt used as a chastity belt. The objects are related, but I'd never seen the connection before.

Russian planes, no matter where they are, all sound as if they are going to Siberia. After I stopped looking for signs of life from the spurned seat-belted woman and the *Granma*-reading bureaucrat, I noticed that the whole plane, except for the Anglos, was making out. The old guy in the seat in front of me was moving on a late-twentyish *señora* next to him, while an ugly crone with a wart on her nose across the isle was studying him with an intense gaze meant, I believe, to smother his passion. I fancied that she was his wife. It was a poetic country: while I tried to meet my observation quota, they were meeting a libidinal one.

SANTIAGO DE CUBA

Situated at the eastern end of the island, Santiago de Cuba is the city of the Revolution. The Sierra Maestra, where Castro's band of guerrillas began its war against the Batista regime, is etched around the city. The faithful used to make pilgrimages to Castro's hideouts and to the small villages that supplied the Revolutionaries. These days, however, one is more likely to find wholly apolitical mountain climbers from abroad testing their skills against the cliffs. Before leaving for Cuba, I'd met a journalist in Baltimore who was taking a mountaineer's vacation in the Sierra Maestra. When I asked him if he planned to do some research at the same time, he emphatically said no. He was going camping and climbing.

It was hotter in Santiago de Cuba than in Havana, and there was a decidedly more tropical feeling in the air. The palms shimmered and the asphalt steamed as we gained the city. We took a taxi to the hotel we'd reserved rooms in, but the place was about five miles outside the city, and it was a dead ringer for a Holiday Inn. It was, in fact, a chain hotel built by a Spanish-Cuban company, a so-called joint venture, for tourists. That wouldn't do, so we headed for the center of the city and checked into the Casa Grande, an old, elegant hotel with a splendid terrace looking over the center square and the cathedral.

Lounging with a Cristal beer on the terrace, under a Titian-blue sky, I felt like a colonial bwana, filled with compassion for the natives who were, however, kept at a safe distance by a phalanx of security guards. From my perch I could see the natives surge, the whole anxious mass of the starving, battering itself against the white wall of my castle. Two young girls, suited in the ubiquitous Lycra that made them look like cats and fruit, were eyeing me from the upper level of the cathedral. When they caught me looking, they made a flurry of friendly and suggestive gestures. One of them caressed her breast like a ripe pear and pursed her lips. Had I made the slightest gesture of encouragement they would have vaulted the ten or fifteen meters separating the church from the hotel, and landed fully palpable on my lap. The taxi drivers clustered around their vintage American cars and Soviet Ladas looked expectantly up as well. In Parque Cespedes young women sat on benches, staring languidly at the terrace like supplicants before a shrine. Only a few couples, enveloped in each other, oblivious like all young lovers, ignored the Casa Grande and did their public Latin lovemaking thing, though I wasn't sure if even this innocent activity was not somehow directed toward my libidinal instincts.

I went for a walk. I was immediately approached by several *jineteros*, but I waved them away. A crazy woman with an outlandish yellow hat declared loudly that I had promised to marry her and that I was reneging on the promise. As I walked away faster, her imprecations became more violent. She accused me of neglecting our children, and cried: "Save my babies! Save my babies!" She was neither young nor old, but overwhelmingly tragic, like an actress in a Greek play. She held out her arms Antigone-like and called on various deities to punish me. The scene greatly amused the cabdrivers and the two policemen hanging with them. The amusement was doubtless at my expense. She must have been a well-known local character, who in her craziness symbolized somehow the relationship of all foreigners to Cuba. Yes, indeed, I had promised to marry her, and if not I then certainly some other foreigner. She was Cuba and I was the United States, and her crazy plea was not without foundation. In six days in Cuba I had seen very few crazy people on the street, compared with, let's say, New York.

I took refuge in the Galería Oriente, but the madness did not stay outside, though the crazy woman did. Displayed along the walls were paintings by the winners of the "X Salón provincial de Artes Plásticos."

Óscar Bayola López's *The Baptism* pictured a decaying monster like the mother alien in *Alien,* crouching in a rain of fluttering dollars surrounded by a bursting world of industrial junk and skulls. The message was as obvious as it was ambiguous. The monster was a monster, but the junk around it was still junk. Political monstrosity and crazed materialism were the only options, linked to each other. Was there a way out?

Fernando Goderich's *Iconography of an Era* depicted an idealized revolutionary romantic with flowing tresses and mournful eyes à la José Martí, surrounded by a dense Boschian mob of crazed, copulating citizens. On Martí's head perched a closed fist trapped in a glass box. The symbolism was intricate: the fist of the Revolution was trapped in glass because the citizens were copulating instead of making revolution. As in the other picture, there was an idealistic core surrounded by ironic reality. Cuba was an island surrounded by danger.

Eleomar Puentes's *The Leopard Has a Coat* displayed a coat of nails being pulled apart by two magnets above a filthy, turdy toilet bowl. Once more, two contending forces were pulling apart the iron ideology, while the real world was shit.

Leos Danys, who was not a winner, parodied a socialist-realist painting of the Soviet era, a perfectly painted ironic scene.

While I was browsing, a bohemian older gent approached. He was an old painter named Sandor.

"You like this stuff?" he asked, obviously displeased. "The young. They think they are painting the truth. Their truth. I will show you my work."

I followed Sandor to another room, where his own paintings lay against a wall. He pulled the canvases out one by one and showed them to me. They were brightly colored symbolic paintings of Santería gods. He explained the precise symbolism of a figure giving birth to worlds of lesser gods and humans.

"This is Chango, the god of fire. He is man and woman. He is the spiritual protector of Afro-Cuba." The hermaphroditic Chango with breasts and penis radiated sensuality. Sandor explained his technique, which consisted of laying on the paint thickly with a spatula.

Sandor had painted murals for both official buildings and churches. The irony here was that the Santería subject was completely official, totally approved. Unlike the anguished work of the younger painters, it was the art version of tourist junk. In fact, he tried to sell me the Chango painting. I would have liked to ask the younger painters what they thought of Sandor, but I already knew. Romanian artists of the 1980s had resorted to the same commentaries in private metaphorical language to express their despair. Their contempt for the folklorist, nationalist productions of their elders was boundless.

In the inner courtyard outside the gallery, I noticed a sculpture of a gun stock with an arrow in it. That was right, too. Cuba now was all attitude and no ammo. It was hard to look at anything and not see it symbolically. This wasn't, I think, just my bias. The makers of things Cuban, especially the artists, made sure that what they did would be viewed metaphorically.

CASA DE YASMINA

I had an important mission to perform in Santiago, and I decided to take care of it right away. Back in New Orleans, I had promised Jack that I would take a package and an envelope full of photographs to his girlfriend, Yasmina.

The taxi driver had to ask directions several times to Yasmina's house, but after some wrong turns through the twisting hillside streets, I arrived in front of the *solare*. The whole family, augmented by a dozen neighbors, poured out of the house as my 1957 Oldsmobile taxi came to a stop.

Alas. Yasmina had just left for the mountains, to pick coffee with her Pioneer group. The Pioneers were helping Cuba meet its coffee quota, a patriotic duty. Nonetheless, I was warmly welcomed. Yasmina's mother, who looked no older than thirty, and her grandmother, also very young-looking, kissed me on both cheeks and invited me inside.

I sat on a small stool, surrounded by the bright eyes of ten family members who queried me closely about Jack. The photographs he had taken were passed from hand to hand, and sighs of wonder and admiration filled the room as image after image of Jack and Yasmina at the beach—some of them quite risqué: Yasmina was topless—filed past. Jack had shown me a snapshot, but here I had my first glimpse of the girl in her own surroundings. She was a child, trying to look more grown-up than she was. She barely had any breasts at all. I was embarrassed. I didn't linger over the shots.

"Tell Jack," Yasmina's mother said, "that he shouldn't stay away much longer. Yasmina is blooming, becoming more beautiful every day. She is waiting for him to come next month for her fifteenth birthday, he promised."

I was quite sure that Jack wasn't coming next month: his business was going through a hard time. But I said instead: "I will be sure to tell him."

I was awash in this family's gratitude thanks to my connection with Jack, on whom their hopes were so visibly pinned. I was also familiar enough with local hospitality to know that the reason I was not offered refreshments was that there weren't any. These people were abjectly poor. The dirt floor was swept clean but the room was bare. A cheap lithograph of the Virgen de la Caridad in a plastic frame adorned the wall. I made them my own gifts of soap and candy, and they were grateful. The one hundred dollars a month Jack sent kept all of them alive. Outside of that, their monthly rations were two pounds of sugar, some cooking oil, two pounds of flour, and a bar of soap.

The women were dressed in simple cotton shifts that had straps over the shoulders and ended just above the knees. Their legs were smooth, black, and long. The mother was a beauty, and the grandmother, in her fifties, could still turn a head or two. One of Yasmina's older sisters breast-fed a plump baby, with her legs crossed. One bare foot with long, flexible toes swung back and forth. There were two other young women whose legs were fetchingly bare. Bare feet are lovely, of course, unless you don't have any shoes. This was the moment to bring out the mysteries of the kingdom of Wal-Mart, I thought to myself. I remembered what Jack had told me about the beautiful bareness of Cubana legs, but I didn't listen. I distributed silk stockings. The women snatched them from me the way the Taino must have gone for the broken mirrors of Columbus's sailors. They ripped the plastic from the boxes, unrolled the coiled silk, and pulled it on in front of me, making me blush as their thighs were revealed to their ends. There was something shiny, rapacious, almost feral in their eyes. The snake had come to Eden. Mr. Sam Walton grinned from his grave. I wished I'd brought shoes.

It was hard to leave. They kept asking me to tell them more things about Jack, about life in New Orleans, about myself. I didn't know Jack all that well, but their desire to know was so great I found myself mumbling some neutral platitudes about the great food in his restaurant (not really!), the fine weather in Louisiana, etc. I had the feeling that I could have married all the females in the family and transported them, babies and all, on the next plane. There were several young men there, too, Yasmina's brothers. They were silent during the entire exchange, and though they smiled, I thought that they were angry. There was trouble ahead, yet. I never did find out what they thought about their little sister's affair with the much older Jack, but I could imagine. What was going to come of the wounded pride of young Cuban men who watched their women go off with foreigners for clothes and food?

THE MOON AND THE FARMERS

exquisite corpse no. 12

No silicone in Cuba
todas chichas are legal tender
the long-legged natives
are not Baader-Meinhof—
the grain is in the granary
the new seeds must be stirred.
This is the farmers' song.

—David Graham and Andrei Codrescu

A full moon was hanging over the Casa Grande terrace. The silhouette of the cathedral was sharply outlined in the sky. A chunky angel with sturdy wings stood between the two towers, looking ready to swoop clumsily down. After Havana's big-city hustle and bustle, Santiago at night seemed like an oasis of tranquility. The day's steady flow of Chinese-made bicycles, pedicabs, burros, lead-spewing Ladas, and vintage American cars had slowed down to a crawl. In the park across the street, only a few long-limbed young women still remained, looking longingly at the terrace where middle-aged foreign objects of desire drank *mojitos* and swallowed pork sandwiches.

The terrace was hopping. David was smoking his end-of-the day cigar and drinking the ritual *mojito,* Hemingway's drink. By coincidence, all the men on the hotel terrace looked like the (older) Hemingway.

One of them was a Canadian farmer who introduced himself after knocking a beer off the table and splattering me with it. He told me that every late fall, after the harvest, he and a couple of pals from Quebec packed suitcases full of Salvation Army clothes ("nothing over a dollar") and headed for Cuba, where "for a shirt you can have a beauty."

I imagined Quebec, buried in snow, and didn't really blame him. As I sat there, contemplating both his parsimony and his lust for life, one of his pals, another red-bearded Canadian Hemingway, said: "Let's have another one for Quentin."

Quentin, it turned out, was the third musketeer. He'd had a heart attack in Hoguin the week before. There was a moment of silence for

Quentin; then the first Hemingway said: "He died fucking." And the other Hemingway nodded gravely: "Good for him."

I felt, somehow, that this was an important juncture in Anglo-Creole history. The image of a dead Canadian farmer expiring in the arms of an Afro-Cuban beauty in the newly eroticized socialist island of Cuba was totemic. The last stage of communism was surrealism. Instead of "Workers of the World, Unite," the new slogan was "Eroticize the Proletariat!" And kill the capitalists in bed.

A local magician went from table to table, pulling scarves out of people's beer bottles. He passed his hands over a couple and then pulled a brassiere from his pocket. The woman shrieked. When he came to our table, Ariel recognized him. His name was Tony; he was Cuba's most famous magician. He was deaf-mute. He looked at Art and handed him a small wooden box with a window at the top. There was a dollar inside. He gestured to Art to open it, and then smiled at me. He handed me an empty goblet to hold, then took it back, turned it over to show everyone that it was empty, then proceeded to pull scarves out of it. He pulled out seven scarves, then a full bouquet of plastic flowers, then . . . my watch. I looked at my bare wrist and gasped. I hadn't felt a thing. Art was sweating profusely, trying to open the simple wooden box. I looked for the magician's sleeves but he didn't have any. He was wearing a short-sleeved shirt. Tiptoeing behind him was a pretty girl, a barefoot waif, who collected money from the delighted victims. Tony the Magician sold Art the wooden box and showed him the secret. I bought one, too, and he showed me as well. It was, of course, the simplest thing in the world, involving no pressure or effort. It was a matter of craft. I have owned this box for some time now and I have tormented endless people with it. Simple as it is, the box proves impossible to open because its simplicity goes against common sense.

"He must have known you were a journalist," Ariel told Art.

"How so?"

"You want to find out all about Cuba, so he gave you a box to open that's so simple it drove you crazy."

"I see," said Art. "Like Cuba. We look for the complexity, but it's the simplicity that drives us crazy."

I disagreed. "That must have been true once. Castro wanted to make a simple world where everyone was equal, well fed, and happy. But in the process everything became complicated. It's no simple box anymore."

"Then how come you can't open it?"

"Because there is a dollar inside and it's hard to think of anything but getting the dollar out? Which causes one to miss the trick?"

Maybe. I did admire the deaf-mute magician's acumen. He had given Art the box with the dollar inside. He had taken my watch. Those were our Yankee symbols: the dollar and the watch. We came from a world of time and money. Tony came from Cuba. Something else operated here. We couldn't quite crack it. Tony'd showed me how to open the box and get the dollar out but he couldn't comment, explain, or give a six-hour speech. He was deaf-mute.

To bed is where I went shortly after this. But I couldn't sleep. The whole island of Cuba crowded about in my head, blowing cigar smoke into the room, making everything even foggier than it was. The only clear spot was a little window I kept wiping with my sleeve to see what was behind it. It was Tony with a Castro beard, sticking out his tongue, trying to speak but nothing came out.

Tony the magician astounds Ariel

DAY EIGHT: "TODAY CASTRO DECLARED CHRISTMAS LEGAL"

exquisite corpse no. 13

Today Castro declared Christmas legal
Legal trash, illegal aliens
hurtling toward the windswept
vistas facing backward toward
Santiago de Cuba
She licks you gently with her moon
and polishes the curves of her *señoritas*
to a fine sheen
fastened to a clasping, marveling barrage,
marvelous fruit of spiritual business

—Ariel Pena, David Graham, Art Silverman, and Andrei Codrescu

On December 16, 1997, Fidel Castro declared Christmas a legal holiday in Cuba, and everyone stayed home from work. People gathered to be photographed under Christmas trees.

THE VIRGIN OF CHARITY

The Virgen de la Caridad watches over the Cuban people, and participates in their history. Legend has it that she was found in the sea by sailors whose lives she saved. Ever since, she has watched over perilous sea journeys and has been worshipped by those who leave Cuba over the water. After being brought to El Cobre, she has left her perch in the mountains above Santiago only three times in Cuban history: at the emancipation from slavery; at the successful conclusion of the wars of independence from Spain; and during Fidel's triumphant march from Santiago to Havana. The Virgen de la Caridad entered Havana with Fidel on January 1, 1959. And now she was going to be carried from her shrine for the fourth time when Pope John Paul II arrived in Santiago de Cuba on January 21, 1998.

We drove up to the sanctuary in the mountains. The Virgin's shrine was inside a small church above the mountain village of El Cobre.

There were only a few pilgrims at the church. The day was tropically bright and the sky was cloudless and intensely blue. The church sat in a powerful silence between the Sierra Maestra mountains. A flower seller dozed by the gate. A few trinket vendors applied themselves lazily to displaying cards and rosaries in our direction.

Inside, the cool darkness was breached by flickering candles. Ariel and I found ourselves in a chapel overflowing with offerings to the Virgin of Charity, laid on two altars and on the walls. One wall was entirely covered with *milagros*, miniature representations of afflicted parts of the body, made out of copper or tin. There were also crutches and prostheses here, left behind by the miraculously cured. A mural on the wall depicted the Virgin saving three sailors from a raging sea. The sailors represented all the races of Cuba: white, mulatto, and black.

Standing above her altars, behind glass, was the Virgin, turning slowly on a small pedestal.

"She is powerful," I commented to Ariel, "a powerful figure draped over a silver chalice. An embroidered robe. An infant with a crown bigger than his head. A beautiful gaze that's quite alive. And she's holding the little bambino Jesus by some clasp on his back. I'm not sure how she's holding him. She has a beautiful bell-shaped dress."

Ariel said: "I think the importance of the Virgin for the Catholic Church, especially during these times of communism, is the difference between this Virgin and all the virgins that have been found in Latin America. This Virgin is holding the child Christ in one hand, and in the other hand she holds the cross, which is a promise, an invitation for people to join the Church. For Cuban Catholics that's quite symbolic, that's very important."

"Right. She's holding two symbols. So she's a prince of the Church holding the cross, which I've never seen before. She's usually got her hands full with the child."

"Yeah. So, if you want, for the more radical church in Cuba, she's not just a mother, but she's an active pursuer of change. She is also a godess of Santería, of Afro-Cuba. And she plays quite a symbolic role in liberation struggles in Cuba. And the church here is the closest alternative, somehow, to an opposition to the atheist regime."

"So we are, in fact, in the headquarters of the opposition."

"Yeah."

"She's a warrior."

"Yeah. She's not just a mother who protects a child. She is always taken in all the battles of independence, slave rebellions. And then to Havana during the Revolutionary years. This year I don't know how that's going to take place, but there's a lot of expectation."

When Ariel said this, we looked up expectantly at the figure floating above us in all her finery and mystery. But she revealed nothing. I felt her power as something that surrounded her, the charged particles of belief that numberless followers brought into her presence. That intensity of souls had congealed into an atmosphere charged with feeling, an "air of tears."[39]

"I understand now why bringing her out when the Pope comes is important," I said, "because people associate her with liberation struggles, so they imagine this time around she will do what she's done throughout history. And it's entirely possible, no?"

Ariel wasn't so convinced, but she was hopeful. "Ummm. I think maybe so. I think people are considering the option of thinking and doing things that have not been ordained by the state. And there is no clear path in Cuba where to go. And the Church somehow resolves that problem in terms of finding new ethics, new morals, that no other philosophy can provide. And it feels almost like, after all those years of Marxist indoctrination, where people were made to feel that they could find heaven on earth through a philosophy, they are sort of now going back to the old idea of finding heaven in, you know, somewhere else."

Ariel's hesitations reflected Cuba's. No one was sure what effect, if any, the Pope's visit might have. Cubans had lost their religious practice and the language that went with it. Ariel, like myself, had been raised (or raised herself) Marxist, which is to say, we possessed a language that didn't translate back into any other ideology or belief, no matter that we'd lost our faith in Marxism, too. There is something wrenching— and this is now part of the crisis affecting the ex-commie world—in trying to transfer the obsolete terms of a former existence into something useful afterward. It's like trying to change useless currency for new money. It doesn't go—*no va*—so you say, like Ariel, "heaven, you know, somewhere else . . ." We knew where commie heaven was, but this other, older, heaven . . . ummm.

"I need to make an offering here," I told Ariel. I stuffed a dollar into a box, and listened to it. "That's the sound of an American dollar going in," I said, but I didn't mean any disrespect by that. I wanted not so much to make an offering, as to proffer an excuse for not being able to believe.

I read the scroll below the Virgin: "Over four centuries the Cubans felt that God was listening to them and protected them when they put their faith in the Virgin who interceded for them before her son, Jesus Christ, who is the same as God."

To the right of the shrine was a crucified Jesus who looked a lot like Che Guevara. Under him, it was written: "It is impossible to know Jesus without loving him and to love him without following him."

I glanced through the offerings people had left. There was an adding machine, dedicated in a handwritten note to El Cobre. Perhaps the owner had done well in business overseas. There were two wine-glasses and a note of gratitude for love found. A painting of the Virgin, painted thickly with naive detail and emotion. A copy of an American citizenship certificate. A photograph accompanied by a note that said: "Fifteen people died making their way to freedom. We want to thank the Virgin for protecting us in the ocean. Signed: Renee and Manuel Sánchez, the only survivors." (In the photo, Renee and Manuel are standing next to Miami Photo.) A pair of round, old-fashioned eyeglasses belonging to a teacher. A toy car accompanied by a framed letter explaining a miracle involving a country road and a small girl. There was a stone in a plastic bag with a scroll sealed next to it. There was a catheter, useful no longer because healing had come. A bracelet woven from dry black hair. A medicine bottle with a message inside. Many *milagros* with faded notes tied to them. A dried flower. More eyeglasses. A small box tied with ribbon. A baseball signed by a team from Guantá-namo, thanking the Virgin for an important victory. Many photos of soldiers in uniform dating back to the beginning of the century. A whole officer's uniform, with a letter of thanks for surviving one of Cuba's many battles. There were many, many locks of hair from lovers who had triumphed over adversity. And many—more of these than anything else—letters thanking the Virgin for the miracle of making it over the water to the United States. There were also letters from exiles who had returned to thank the Caridad in person. And other, more ambiguous notes, where hearts had been poured out.

Ariel read a recent one: "This is twenty-fifth of November, 1997. I, a Spanish traveler, ask you, Virgin, to stop the misery of these extraordinary people, so that the next time I come here, they treat me like a person, and not like a mere holder of dollars. I ask you for those who think an idea is more important than a life, who think that an idea is the only thing to live for and die. I ask you to open their eyes, so that they accept that they are mistaken. I ask, Virgin, for this island, for this music, and for its future. And I ask you so that we, the seekers of paradises, can still find a Cuba."

We, the seekers of paradises. It was quite moving.

Looking at the letters and offerings left for the Virgin, I felt (without believing) the power of people's belief in miracles, forgiveness, and favors. I felt alien and ashamed. Alien because neither the fervor nor the hunger of these people was truly mine. I came from a place with supermarkets and drugstores, heat and electricity—those miracles I took for granted. And ashamed because the food and medicine so easily available to me were denied to the people of the Virgin de la Caridad by the craziness of their government and mine. Nothing in my Wal-Mart bag seemed *personal* enough to leave the Virgin. I had rarely felt more like a stranger, and I have been one for much of my life. I was, in fact, very much in need of a miracle. I bought some flowers and placed them at the feet of the small figure in the glass case. Ariel averted her eyes.

HAVANA, Jan. 23 (Associated Press)—The Virgin of Charity, which Pope John Paul II will crown on Saturday, claims the devotion of many Cubans, either as the Catholic patron saint of the nation, as a goddess of Afro-Cuban beliefs, or as both. Many Cubans have a replica of El Cobre's Virgin of Charity in their homes, a few saying Roman Catholic prayers to her and many more adoring her as Ochun, the goddess of love, rivers and gold in the "Santería" belief, a religion brought by slaves from Africa that incorporates some Christian elements. The great majority of Cubans are considered followers of Santería and other Afro-Cuban religions, including many of the four million—out of a population of 11 million—officially considered Roman Catholics. For the first time in 30 years of communist rule under President Fidel Castro, the Virgin of Charity will be taken out of her sanctuary in the village of El Cobre, to be presented to the pope. The pope, who is on a five-day tour of Cuba, will crown the Virgin in the nearby southeastern city of Santiago de Cuba, where he will celebrate mass on Saturday. Parallels are being drawn with a similar celebration in 1979, when John Paul II paid tribute to Poland's venerated Black Madonna during a visit to his native land that was seen as contributing to the downfall of communism in Eastern Europe. In her enclosure in El Cobre, the small statue turns slowly on her pedestal—thanks to an electric motor. She alternately faces a grand altar and a more intimate sanctuary where the faithful gather, in an about-face symbolic of her dual personality. Below the steps leading to the Virgin's chapel, in a grotto darkened by candle smoke, her admirers, many of whom believe she holds magic powers, present their offerings. Her wealth, according to the chronicles of the sanctuary, includes a small gold statue offered by Castro's mother to show her gratitude for keeping her revolutionary son alive. U.S. author Ernest Hemingway, who fished, drank and wrote in Cuba, gave her the medal that came with his Nobel Literature prize. The Archbishop of Santiago de Cuba declared El Cobre's Virgin of Charity the patron saint of Cuba in 1936, after veterans of the independence war against Spain made the request. The veterans had written to Pope Benedict XV, saying that in combat, "when death and desperation approached, this vision of the Virgin emerged always, as a light dissipating all danger."

After the darkness of the church, the sky outside was particularly blinding. I bought more flowers to take back with me. A beautiful young woman was buying flowers, too.

"What are you asking from the Virgin?"

"Health for my child," she said. "Also . . . a successful resolution to my love situation."

Her name was Serafina.

When I pressed her for details, she pointed to a young man who sat on a stone ledge, watching us, smiling. "Ask him," Serafina said.

Alonso was a thirty-five-year-old Spaniard who had been pursuing Serafina's love.

"I came to Cuba a year ago," Alonso explained. "I chose Cuba randomly. I came with a cousin of mine. We were having beers and I met her."

"Did you go back to Spain after that?"

"Yeah. I had to leave after those three days. I had to go to Havana. Then we kept in touch. Phone calls. Two months later I was back in Santiago."

"What was it about her that Spanish girls didn't have?"

"I don't know, but there was something."

"Is it something about Cuban girls?"

"To tell you the truth, I don't know. This relationship has difficulties. I can think of easier relationships. Letters take a month and a half. Very difficult. There is a mysterious force in these girls that attracts me."

"Are you able to help her financially? What is her situation?"

"Her financial situation is very difficult. I don't understand the Cuban economy. In Spain people ask me why I am sending such a large amount of money here. Salaries are so small here."

"How much do you send, and how often?"

"It depends. Sometimes two hundred dollars."

"Supports her whole family?"

Alonso laughed.

"Yeah, her husband, too, and her two children. But really, I've not only found a woman . . . but a whole family. Her family. Her cousin is like my brother. I found a family."

"So what about the future? Can you live in Cuba, or can she live in Spain?"

"Our plans are for her to go to Spain. But there are bureaucratic problems. If a common relation between a common man and woman can be hard, you can imagine this one."

"Do you think that the fact you can't be together adds to the romance?"

"Yes. I once fancied a girl. I wrote poems to her. My mom said, 'You are lying to her. You are making her believe you are romantic. But you are a porcupine.'"

"A porcupine?"

We had a laugh over this one, trying to figure out what precise meaning "porcupine" had in the fields of romance. The best we could come up with was that it was prickly, antisocial, and hard to know. On the other hand, Alonso's pursuit of Serafina seemed quite romantic. Unless there was something I had missed.

"Are there many Spanish men with Cuban women?"

"Yeah. Quite a lot. In Leone, where I live, quite a few have gotten together."

"Is this a way for Spain to take back the old colony a woman at a time?"

Alonso laughed. "Yes. Cuba is the most loved ex-colony of Spain. I think you're right, there is a mystery."

"Maybe that explains the mystery of your attraction to Serafina."

"Just a little bit."

Later, I found out that the Spanish embassy in Havana was running a matchmaking service. Cuban girls brought their photos to the embassy to be forwarded to Spanish men wanting to meet Cuban women. Long lines of Cuban girls formed around the embassy from early in the morning until closing time. Many Cuban girls married the men in absentia, then left Cuba to be with their husbands. It costs $625 for a marriage license, and the state will even throw in a little ceremony at La Maison, a kitschy mansion in Havana. De Quesada, a Spanish diplomat in charge of issuing visas for Cuban women, has approved thousands of them over the years, refusing only two. He did so once when a twenty-four-year-old woman who was marrying a ninety-two-year-old man admitted that she was not in love. He also refused a fourteen-year-old who was marrying a thirty-six-year-old man with whom she'd had sex since she was thirteen. Sexual relations at that age are illegal both in Cuba and Spain.[40]

Other Europeans had gotten the word on Cuba's latest export, but for the Spanish something more was involved. As I'd told Alonso half in jest, Spain would like to take Cuba back woman by woman. That is, if the Americans didn't get into the act soon, as they always seemed to do at critical moments in Cuban-Spanish history. And then Cuban boys and men would find their national pride . . . and the wheel would turn again.

After leaving the sanctuary of the Virgin, we stopped briefly at the convent of El Cobre, where Fidel Castro stayed for two weeks at the end of the year 1958 while waiting for his guerrilla army to clear the way for his triumphal entry into Havana.

Myself and the Spaniard's girl

The Spaniard's girl

Sister María, who guarded the gates, told us that a retreat for university students was in progress, and that we must walk very softly as to not disturb them. We tiptoed through the flower-filled courtyard, past the small doors of cells where students meditated. Sister María pointed to door 66, behind which Fidel had awaited word from his troops. The nun who had fed and cared for him was still alive, at age eighty-eight. Ariel's husband, Tom, had interviewed her for the BBC. I

The Convent of El Cobre, where Fidel stayed before marching on Havana

**The singing girls
(Cobre Convent)**

would have liked to see the room, to feel its vibrations. But, oddly, a student was in there.

"I thought that all Cuban students were atheist," I whispered to Sister María.

She smiled. "That was true . . . once."

Outside, on the steps of the convent, we met Sister Rita with five little girls. She had brought them to sing at the convent, but the silent retreat had canceled the plan. I asked them to sing for us instead.

The little girls' sweet voices singing "Ave Maria" soared through the tropical afternoon. Their freshly scrubbed faces shone with an innocence and joy that knew nothing as yet of Spanish men, rickety rafts atop dangerous waves, or tear-stained locks of hair left before the Virgin of Charity.

I gave them each a pencil from Wal-Mart. The pencils had the logos of American baseball teams on them. I wished they were magic pencils, though, and that honey and milk might flow from them instead. Back in Santiago, we spotted more and more signs marking the imminent arrival of the Pope. The government had issued an official flier of the Pope shaking hands with Castro. The image was also marketed on T-shirts, a stroke of entrepreneurial genius. In souvenir-free Cuba, this was a real find. Something about the placement of the Pope signs suggested that he was expected to accomplish miracles. Across the street from the cathedral, I saw a man running from Parque Cespedes shouting: "The Pope is coming! Cubans will be free! Wake up!" Two bemused

Waiting for the Pope

policemen looked at him without moving: he must have been the local idiot. He was not the only one: a retarded boy with jerky energy
screamed at a group of taxi drivers who were teasing him: "The Pope
will punish you!" They laughed, along with the policemen. Everyone
looked forward to the Pope's visit, but without much attending awe.
This was no Poland. Most people planned to attend, marching a few
miles from their towns to the Pope's speaking sites. The one place the
Pope would not be preaching was Santiago's Che Guevara Square, in
deference to Che's atheism. The Church had publicized the event from
the pulpits, but it had been allotted no photocopying machines or computers to spread the word. The Communists feared the printed word, a
primal fear that went back to the roots of the ideology, which had been
formed in illegal printshops. In Romania, typewriters were registered
with the police until Ceauşescu's last day.

Inside the seventeenth-century Santiago cathedral, two young student painters were restoring a seventeenth-century Spanish Jesus. The
statue was lying on its back while the meticulous brushwork gave life to
his toes. The young restorers were doing their work with good grace,
managing simultaneously to flirt with a pretty student who perched on
a decommissioned baptismal fountain with her legs crossed over a very
short skirt.

"Is he going to be ready by January twentieth?" That was the day of
the papal visit.

"I don't think so." The young woman laughed, "These two can't
keep their minds on their work."

The cathedral's most remarkable feature was an extraordinarily
bloody Virgen del Dolores with a bloody knife through her heart. She
looked almost serene within the jets of blood shooting from the wound.
To the left of her was a prominently displayed bomb-shelter symbol,
dating, I thought, from the days of the Cuban missile crisis.

The Eighth Day ended with a ride in a pedicab. This was a bicycle
with a wide backseat, powered by a skinny guy with hairy stick legs who
panted frightfully while pulling on a homemade cigar. I had to dis-
mount several times to help him up the hill, until he finally gave up.

When I returned to Casa Grande, everyone was in a festive mood.
For the first time since 1959, Cubans were openly celebrating Christmas. Christmas trees had sprouted everywhere, a forest of twinkling
lights that covered the island.

DAY NINE: A DAY WITHOUT A CORPSE

The day dawned beautifully over Casa Grande. A good night's sleep had me up early. I walked to a charming park by the waterfront. Two rusted tugboats were sinking quietly at the rotten pier. There was a wooded, hilly island in the bay, and the blue mountains in the distance were Japanese misty.

The Santiago Market, state run, was already bustling. All the stalls with signs that read "Eggs" or "Meat" were empty. The only food was a mound of rotten bananas, a pile of cabbages, a pyramid of manioc roots, some sorry-looking potatoes, and some shriveled oranges. Nonetheless, an energetic crew of housewives with plastic bags were loading up on these peso items. Somewhere there was a private market holding the better-looking portions of these crops, along with the missing eggs and meat—for dollars.

The banana guy at the state market in Santiago

In front of the not-yet-open Santiago Cigar Factory, a few *jineteros* were at work already. "I sell you cigars," a fifteen-year-old in a muscle shirt said. "You want to go inside, it will be twice as much. You want cigars, I go inside, bring them out, half the price."

"Why aren't you in school?" I asked.

"Why? Waste my peak earning years?"

Jinetero = smart-ass. See you in Miami.

Two fat guys—unusual Cubans—walked by clad in T-shirts that said "Miss Deaf Ohio" and "Miss Deaf Cleveland." What Midwestern yard sale had generated these shirts, and how did they get onto these backs? I remembered the Canadian Hemingway's "one shirt, one girl," and wondered if these guys'd had sex with tourists so they could dress up in these messages. Or had their girls, to dress *them* up? Art had brought his "Earth Day 1992" and "Johns Hopkins Bookstore" T-shirts to give away, but still had them packed in his suitcase. I think he was afraid to give them to anybody because the gesture might have been misinterpreted. He might have handed them innocently to some tough guys and then been required to run when they insisted on paying up.

I gave some of the T-shirts I'd brought to David, our new driver. Like Arturo in Havana, David lived well on the proceeds of his vintage

Our driver's daughter

David and family

Oldsmobile—and, perhaps, on information he provided to the appropriate organs. But he was a very nice guy.

BILL AND SHEILA

We met Bill on the terrace of the Casa Grande. He was an American living in Santiago who liked to frequent the tourist hotels to meet fellow Americans for conversation. A compact, strong, Brooklyn-born Italian-American in his late fifties, Bill had come to Cuba via Jamaica, where he'd run a bar. He had fallen in love with a Cuban girl, had sold his bar, and moved in with her, in defiance of the embargo, the Helms-Burton Act, and the accumulated wisdom of history.

We began talking with Bill about food. I asked him about a place that advertised Italian food. "Yeah," Bill said, "Italian food just like my mother used to throw up.

"I was raised in Brooklyn, had seventeen brothers and sisters. I had a bar in Jamaica, just sold it. I've been coming to Cuba for fifteen years, then one day I said to myself, That's it, Bill, you're fifty-seven years old, you have to settle down. So I did. My wife is twenty-two years old; we have a baby. I brought all my Sonys here, we have the biggest TV on the block. We are popular."

Bill was unapologetic and full, equally, of contempt for U.S. policy toward Cuba, and enthusiasm for the future.

"I'd like every American to come over. Helms-Burton is shit. The potential here is unbelievable. But the authorities have tunnel vision. I want to open a bar. . . . It will be the best goddamned bar they've ever seen, right here in the center. But they have trouble reentering the business world. They need expertise. They need to know what tourists want . . . what Germans want, what Italians want. The bureaucracy is impossible."

What will happen, I wanted to know, when U.S. tourists do come?

"It could be terrible. If they come only looking for Cuban women, it's no good. That's happening now, because there is no money. Money will flow here. My big fear is that the drug man will come right behind tourism. There are no drugs in Cuba now. There are family values here."

Take that, Jesse Helms.

Bill invited us to his home. The house sat on a hillside street of small, pastel-colored buildings, some with tiny balconies. There were flowerpots in front of the houses. Kids played stickball on the streets with their dads and older brothers, women sat on steps smoking and talking, small kids ran their bikes down the middle of the carless road, old men played dominoes that clicked like skeletal insects. A radio played a sentimental song, and a girl on a balcony looked dreamily far away somewhere to the water where her love tourist might one day come. A soccer game wafted out of a television set, and the voices of the men watching it rose at muffled intervals in little sound puffs like cartoon balloons. There was an ease at the heart of this street that made me nostalgic for something I barely recalled, childhood in Sibiu in the safe Stalinist days of poverty, family, and silence. The frequent black-outs helped: they came every other day. "But not in military or diplomatic buildings," Ariel whispered. The houses themselves look like toys to my American-trained eyes, but they were no *solares*.

"This is Cuban middle-class," explained Bill. "The manager of the telephone company lives across the street, the head of the tourism bureau is over there. . . . They are yuckies."

Young Urban Cuban Communists. "On twenty dollars a month?" I asked.

"Some of them get money from relatives in Miami. But everybody's pretty much the same . . . the only difference is their job."

Sheila, whose original name was Yalin, beamed when we were introduced. She was holding Bill Junior in her arms, a gorgeous café con leche Cuban-American who seemed most interested in our presence. Sheila's father, mother, and brother were all smiles, too. Bill relished the introductions and basked in the family warmth. The father retired discreetly, and Bill said: "He's an educated man. An army captain, was with the Bearded One in the Revolution."

We sat in a tiny living room dominated by Bill's thirty-six-inch Sony television. A small statue of the Virgen de la Caridad was on top of it. On the wall, two oil landscapes of tropical paradise were joined by a Christmas wreath. Bill installed himself in the big papa chair—the only one in the room—and surveyed his domain with satisfaction. Crouching at his feet was Hooker the dog, brought over from Jamaica. "The only Hooker allowed in the bar," he quipped.

I sat across from Bill on a plastic bucket seat. Sheila remained standing, holding her baby.

"How did you meet Bill, Sheila?"

She laughed a little-girl laugh and looked proprietarily at him. "He was so drunk. When he met me, I speak English the same. After six months he bring me to Jamaica. Then we plan to marry."

"I met her at the hotel one night. She was the prettiest girl in the place," says Bill. "Married last year. Had a son. My first marriage."

"Did you feel at home right away?"

Bill settled even deeper in the papa chair. "I was surprised at the treatment. You would think that after a forty-year embargo the Cubans would be mad. If my fellow Yanks came down here to see, they'd go home and tell Congress to end this nonsense."

Sheila, I noticed, held herself like a dancer. There was both ease and pride in her carriage. I had noticed this in other Cuban women, who carried themselves with an unself-conscious authority. I wondered aloud what Cuban men thought of foreigners raiding the shores of the fair isle.

"Everyone is happy for me," Sheila answered, and if there was a school chum or a fellow Pioneer somewhere behind her bright eyes, I couldn't see him. Well, maybe, just maybe, Cuban women, unlike any others on earth, did love balding, middle-aged men for themselves, not for their money. Maybe thirty-eight years of holding up Castro and Hemingway as role models have given Cuban girls a real daddy complex. Bill was a wonderful guy: witty, smart, virile, worldly.

"What's a typical day like for you?" I asked Bill.

"Finding items to put on the dinner plate. Cubans survive ninety percent on pork. I'm dying for ravioli and spaghetti."

Bill returned, insistently, to one of his obsessions. "I'm waiting for Cuba to become the Paris of the Caribbean again. There are untouched beautiful buildings, great fishing, the coral reef is intact. . . . It's nearly gone in the Bahamas. Today there was no electricity . . . so what. I played stickball on the street. Played with my baby."

"He likes my family," said Sheila. "He spoke to them, they liked him. I was born here. My friends are here. I like this place."

"What did they teach you in school about the United States?"

"Only the bad side. No talking much about the people. I have plenty friends Cuban in the U.S.A."

And that, of course, was the constant other side of this story of Cubans and Americans. Almost every Cuban has family or friends in the U.S.A. Loving and marrying an American may be a little like reuniting with loved ones on the other side of the water. On the street, every *jinetero*'s first question was "Where are you from? Italy? Canada?

Spain?" And when you said, "Estados Unidos," they shouted for joy. "Estados Unidos? My father is in Miami! My brother is in New York! My sister is in Cleveland!"

There weren't many Americans living with Cuban women in Santiago de Cuba. Bill knew only two. "A guy from Philadelphia . . . an engineer . . . lives near the cathedral . . . and a guy from Phoenix. But there are plenty with girlfriends who come for a week or two . . . send money."

This would surely change when the embargo came down.

David had wandered down the street to take some pictures and had met everybody. We were invited into another house, two doors down from Bill's. It was a pristine and tasteful two-story dwelling, home to three proud and graceful women, a mother and two daughters. The oldest daughter was betrothed to a Spaniard, and was awaiting her visa for Spain. She had classic Spanish features. She sat proudly beneath an old-fashioned wedding photo of her parents, in a wooden frame, and

Bill, Sheila, and Bill, Jr.

Sheila

answered questions calmly, methodically, and properly. On the subject of love she was oddly calm.

"Do you miss him?" I asked.

"Yes, of course, but I will see him in six months." I got the feeling that this was a liaison of convenience—that her Spaniard, whoever he was, was her job for the family. She was seventeen, but her younger sister, fifteen, extraordinarily beautiful (as was the mother), laughed at some of her sister's pronouncements. Then she asked David, who reminded her (of course) of John Travolta: "How old are you? Are you married?"

When David said yes, she turned to Art: "How about you?" Then to me. She was a flirt and much warmer than her sister, who looked at her without expression, with only a very slight narrowing of the eyes.

"Many of these girls," Ariel later told me, "divorce their men when they get to Spain, and become prostitutes."

Indeed—after life in Cuba, it must be difficult to settle down into the severe rhythms of provincial Spanish life, especially if love isn't particularly the case. These girls craved excitement, the glitter of the material world, everything they'd never had in Cuba. On the wall of the small room was a series of odd photos of babies with birds on their heads. A clean, colonial, García Márquez–tinted atmosphere surrounded the three women. There were no men around.

Waiting bride

We said our good-byes to the whole street. Bill and Sheila, with Bill Junior grinning widely, waved good-bye as our car pulled away. The three women waved daintily. Several others, who had introduced themselves much too quickly, blew us kisses. I had the feeling of a world in motion, pulled by centrifugal forces in all directions, but kept in place somehow by Bill the American, who by settling here had given it renewed stability. But isn't that the way it is everywhere? The stranger renews our sense of place. (If not our faith in it, exactly.)

We ate lunch in the dark at Paladar de Mireya, recommended by Bill. The electricity blackout hadn't stopped business at the *paladar.*

Several people were waiting. Eating fish in the hot, moist dark, shooing away swarms of flies from the food, was surely a recipe for disaster. We were sitting on a bench in the tiny room, approximating the locations of our mouths. I missed and scattered rice down the front of my shirt. The fish had a lot of bones, and I picked my way through most gingerly. How long had this place been without electricity? How long had this fish been waiting unrefrigerated? "Don't worry," Art said, reading my mind, "it's well fried." Curiously enough, given all the odd meals at odd hours in odd places, I didn't get sick in Cuba at all.

Santiago's Casa de Cultura, like the House of Culture of my youth, was where the glories of national culture were displayed. There were some distinct differences between the Cuban and the Romanian versions. When our little crew arrived in the marbled hall, the small but enthusiastic crowd, which had come to see the Grupo Folklórico Casumbi and its two female dancers, was well on its way to delirium. Several bottles of rum passed from hand to hand, putting the rum in rumba. I took a careful swig when it was offered. The band played with gusto for a few minutes; then its leader took the stage and offered a lecture on the history and importance of rumba. After the interminable speech, during which the mostly middle-aged crowd fidgeted and drank, the band started up again. A long-legged dancer went into action, but no sooner had the band gotten in the groove than the leader stepped up again to make another edifying speech. The music resumed and the other dancer went into puppetlike action. This went on for a while. Song. Speech. Song. Speech. The speeches were longer than the songs and dances. The audience dutifully applauded both. Rum *et circenses*— without *panis*. The Folkloric Ethos was in bloom, just as in the culture house of my youth, but then there had been no rum, and our dancers hadn't been this hot. And the music: the music hadn't been rumba.

Later that evening, in search of music, we went to Casa de los Estudiantes, which we'd been told catered to Cubans, not tourists. The cavernous hall was crammed with a hot, dense crowd of young Cubans who jerked spastically to . . . American disco music. There was a thick smell of sweat, rum, and sperm. It was fifteen degrees hotter inside, and it was hot outside. Here was the Great Unwashed!

As I shoved my way to the tin bar, a drunk one-eyed pugilist with one arm around an unusually ugly girl put his lips right next to my ear and slurred in fairly good English: "I'm buying you a drink." I declined, because I had just ordered an unopened bottle of rum from the hostile waitress. An unopened bottle involved a trip to the back. Drunk boys pressed against me on all sides, handing empty beer cans and plastic jugs to a waitress who filled all containers from a hose connected to a barrel of rum. There was no more beer.

"No," the pugilist said belligerently, dropping his arm from around the girl and laying it heavily on my shoulders, "I have money. I buy you a drink. I was in Miami. Capitalism sucks. Fucking Americans." It was the first open expression of hostility against Yanks that I'd encountered in Cuba. "I was there. Three years. I come back because I love my sister!" He pushed the scared-looking teenager toward me. "You wanna fuck her?"

I declined again and tried to ignore him. I had the feeling that he'd left Miami in a hurry. "Juvenile delinquent" was written all over him. Probably did time, too. My bottle arrived and I paid. He whirled around and looked as if he were about to get me with an uppercut, but he was drunk and one-eyed, so I retreated into the crowd moving in the dark to the sweaty American disco and, gathering my comrades, beat it out of there.

Out on the street, I perceived for the first time the existence of a deep, hard anger under the smiley face Cuba shows tourists. I'd known it was there, it had to be, but I hadn't put a face to it. Doubtless, it had many faces, but the one I'd seen was the face of a hardened Marielito who'd found no love in the promised land. He was back in Cuba now with a working knowledge of the enemy. He would be one of the first to enlist on the nationalist side of a civil war, the first to hurl himself into the fire for his ugly sister, for Cuba's honor, for the humiliation he had suffered. I thought of the Russian writer Edward Limonov, whose book, *It's Me, Eddie,* written on the fire escape of a flophouse in Times Square, was a cri de coeur against the evils of capitalism. When he returned to Russia after the collapse of the USSR, Limonov translated his failure in the West into a political party called the Bolshevik-Nationalist Party, which swore revenge on the West. Limonov himself rode in Bosnia with the Serbian irregulars, brandishing an automatic weapon, calling for blood. There was some educational difference between the one-eyed drunk pugilist in the Casa de los Estudiantes and the published Russian author, but not much.

The sense of menace dissipated somewhat as we walked. Swarms of young women in Lycra miniskirts, short shorts, and high platforms swarmed us. The most persistent *chicas* were two teenagers whose endowments burst out of clumsily tied scarves, and a miniskirted beautician in training. They cajoled, purred, and demanded that we take them inside a disco. Art asked Ariel to tell them that we would pay their way in, but that once they were in there, we had nothing but honorable and voyeuristic intentions. This they fervently promised, and we paid the two-dollar fee for them. I remembered, of course, Jack's admonishment, "Once you pick a girl, she's yours," but I didn't want to believe it.

The disco was actually a garden restaurant with a small dancing stage on which a salsa band did its thing. Every chair was occupied by three or more people, mostly a tourist plus the three Cubanas on his lap. The tables were toppling under dozens of bottles of beer, soft drinks, and *mojito* glasses. Most of the girls looked thirteen and were drinking soft drinks, either because they weren't allowed to have rum, or because they were taking antibiotics for the clap. This uncharitable thought entered my head when the Lycra-suited beautician, who had attached herself to my lap, ordered an orange soda. She looked old enough to drink, especially after she'd told me that she had a five-year-old bambino at home. The other two girls had arrayed themselves across Art and David's laps and were wiggling their butts to my friends' great discomfort.

Art, who fancied himself a great dancer, extricated himself from the wiggle by pulling the girl onto the dance floor. Here, however, dance rules unknown to us prevailed. The dark bodies on the stage did not move in any familiar fashion: the women unwound upward like "electric eels" (as Ariel put it), while molding themselves around the men. Art was working valiantly at following the rhythm of the music, but his partner had glued her behind to him, drawing him onto her active buttocks and back like a human plunger. Art was dragged helplessly behind her, shaken like a rag doll by an adhesive force greater than his mere will. When they returned to the table, drenched in sweat, David said drily: "Sorry, no paper towel." But then it was his turn. The teenager, who had already decided that he was none other than John Travolta, dragged his sorry ass to the dance floor and did the flypaper thing on him.

I refused to budge. My chair was under a big ceiba tree with fat roots, and I held fast between them. My beautician tried in vain to shake me loose from the ceiba. After dancing a few rounds on her own and returning, she finally said to Ariel (although we'd been getting along fine in Spanish): "Tell him that I want to sleep with him." Ariel laughed and translated this into English. Meanwhile, the vixen laid a hand way up in my lap. "Tell her," I said, shaking loose, "that I am queer." Ariel translated this, but something about my statement sounded unconvincing, because her grip became firmer. I realized that I had, unwittingly, made some kind of commitment, so I pulled out five dollars and placed it in her hand, which loosened its grip reluctantly. This was fully the price of a sexual act plus a full-length life story, but now it turned out that my friend genuinely liked me and decided to be offended. She no longer spoke to me, but to Ariel, asking her to translate. In short, she said that she really liked me, that she was sorry that all I thought of Cuban women was that they were whores, and that I didn't know what I was missing. I asked Ariel to offer my apologies, and to say that if I had had any attraction to women, she would have been the first to benefit. The exchange of chivalrous regrets, which sounded very Spanish to me somehow, did not prevent my injured suitor from taking the five dollars. She had, after all, a five-year-old child.

Art and David tried, with considerable more difficulty, to extricate themselves from their dance partners. It took, I think, ten dollars each, and many expressions of social outrage at the breach of manners.

"Is it only my impression," I said to Ariel, "that they speak a very odd Spanish?"

"It's true," Ariel said. "Cuban Spanish is not very pretty. They drop half the words, and the farther east you go, the more they drop."

After we went back to Casa Grande, I couldn't sleep. The idea that the streets were still alive out there was drawing me. I could feel their pulse. I looked out my little balcony. The moon was full. Parque Cespedes squirmed like an anthill, and an intoxicating scent of tropical blooms and sweat rose up. The sounds of several bands wafted in from the still-open bars. I got dressed again.

DR. SYLVIA

Clubo 300 at four-thirty a.m. was full of astonishingly well-dressed and good-looking people. I thought for a moment that I had gone through a hole in the earth and ended up at a Miami coke club. I sat at the bar, ordered a beer, and caught, immediately, the attention of a sophisticated couple. The very handsome man smiled and introduced himself. He was Roberto, an engineer with a joint-venture energy company. He gave me a lighter with his company logo on it. This alone gave

Girls waiting outside
disco in Santiago

Rumba group

me pause. A Cuban making me a present of a lighter? Disposable though it was, this lighter was yet an invaluable commodity. Such largesse called for a round of drinks, so I offered to buy him and his lovely wife one. He accepted, but the wife, who smiled distantly and politely, did not. After Roberto took a sip from his drink, he swooped his mate off her seat and engaged her in a sinuous, slow dance with his hand on her butt—placed there, I thought, for my benefit. Once, during the dance, she caught my eye, and I shuddered. She wore a black dress with shoulder straps. The tops of her breasts were a shiny warm tan and her shoulders were classically elegant. The dress stopped a few inches above her knees, enough to suggest that the long legs in high heels tapered upward with seductive knowledge.

When the dance was over, Roberto introduced her. "This is Sylvia. She takes care of these people." He made an inclusive gesture that took in all the good-looking people in the bar. I asked who they were, and the mystery finally cleared. The clientele consisted of professional dancers at the Tropicana nightclub. Sylvia was the troupe's doctor. Every workplace in Cuba, even traveling work teams, had its own doctor-in-residence. Of course, they had no medicines.

Sylvia took her aloof stool at the bar, and I kept buying drinks for Roberto, who regaled me with enthusiastic details of his workplace, a modern company that had shiny computers and paid real wages. I was glad for him, but I couldn't take my eyes off Sylvia, who looked at some point behind the bar as if spotting small silver aliens in the bar-length mirror.

When Roberto left me to go the bathroom, I looked at Sylvia, but she was gone. I spotted her at the end of the bar, talking to a waitress. A few moments later, the waitress came over and slipped me a note. I put it quickly into my pocket because Roberto had returned. Soon after, I went to the bathroom myself. The note, dictated by Sylvia, and translated and written by the waitress, read:

> If you want call me tomorrow at 92365—Me name is Sylvia I'm
> a Doctor—please

I returned to the table and bought Roberto more drinks. Sylvia passed by me once, brushing me lightly with her hair. It sent a tingle all the way to my toes. She smelled warm and silky beneath the cocktail dress. I picked a furled red rose that had mysteriously appeared on the bar in front of me, and I licked the tip of it. Luckily, Roberto had been looking elsewhere. All of this took but a brief second. I could see through the slats on the door that it was daytime already. I invited both of them to the Casa Grande terrace for breakfast. It was too early for breakfast, but we had coffee, and I had occasion to study both of them in the daylight. I hadn't been wrong. Sylvia didn't speak much, and barely glanced at me, but her black hair and shoulders were even more royally alluring. The royally drunk Roberto slurred whole paragraphs in what he imagined to be English. Finally, Sylvia took his car keys and led him down the marble steps of the Casa Grande. At the bottom of the stairs, knowing full well that I was staring at her, Sylvia turned and a fleeting smile touched her lips. Tomorrow, then.

DAY TEN: "THE DICTATORSHIP OF THE PROLETARIAT HAS COLLAPSED"

exquisite corpse no. 14

the dictatorship of the proletariat
has collapsed & salt is unnecessary.
"Bolus," she cried, removing her torso.
The perfect shape of womanhood
puts the tree into perspective.
I thought that the thing he was holding
era lo que yo deseaba en ese momento.

—Ariel Pena, David Graham, Art Silverman, and Andrei Codrescu

Sylvia showed up for her six p.m. appointment dressed nicely in high-heeled shoes and a not-too-short clingy black dress. I waited for her across the street from Clubo 300, sitting on a stone ledge with other stone-ledge traffic watchers. Two guys passed a bottle back and forth. One wizened fellow stopped to show me a paper bag full of handmade cigars. People glanced at me in passing but I was relatively unhassled.

Sylvia had come directly from work: her hand, which I kissed European-style, smelled strongly of disinfecting scrub soap. We went to the rooftop *terraza* of the Casa Grande. The cathedral spires were outlined dramatically in the blue-dark of the twilight sky, the chunky angel firmly planted between them. We had rum. The canciones on the loud-speaker were all *canciones de amor.* "Bese me querida/bese me mucho." Her coffee-colored skin was like a soft fabric agitated by a sea breeze. Suddenly, it was evening. Below us lay Santiago de Cuba with its sparse lights and I could no longer make out the ridges of the Sierra Maestra beyond.

My companions had commandeered a table nearby and were treating Bill and Sheila to dinner and drinks. I could hear snatches of their conversation and laughter, but the moonlight buried all of them in a gauzelike transparency.

My Spanish was fading, and the doctor's English was nonexistent. Every time I looked at her she rippled like water traversed by a current. I watched her walk away to make a telephone call.

I asked her to spend the night.

She couldn't afford to be seen with a tourist, Dr. Sylvia said. In any case, she wouldn't be allowed in my room at the Casa Grande. This seeming difficulty was solved by our cabdriver, David, who suggested the name of a nearby *paladar*. It was about half a block away, in a peeling but still ornate pre-Revolutionary building. We climbed up a dark curving stairway to the first landing and rang the buzzer.

The landlady was a pleasant, middle-aged woman who took her time, chatting all the while with Dr. Sylvia about the deprivations of every day. This, I thought, was nervous chatter meant to assuage Sylvia's conscience, but the landlady didn't care. She not only approved, she was most encouraging. Nor did she leave us immediately alone after she showed us the high-ceilinged, pleasant room, with its bed, couch, night table, and mirror. She lowered her bulk onto the couch as we scouted the chamber, and continued her litany. I think she was lonely and was using the polite conventions to wrest a little of our time for herself. I gave her twenty-five dollars for the night and she wrote a receipt slowly, still talking about blackouts, prices, lack of food. Like elsewhere in Cuba, there was no awkwardness about sex, no prudishness.

When the landlady finally left, Sylvia sat next to me on the couch and kept talking through the small preliminaries. As I slipped the dress off her shoulder, she explained that she was better paid than most doctors in Cuba, about twenty dollars a month, because she was assigned to the dancers of the Tropicana Club, a wealthy business. When I kissed the large dark nipples she told me that the only way Cubans survived was by helping each other. Families and strangers shared what they had and traded what they could. When her dress came off and she stood in her black lace panties she told me that her ten-year-old daughter was being cared for tonight by her mother, and that her family lived together in her small house. She told me that she practiced her craft without medicines because none were available in Cuba, and it was only when my fingers met and caressed the dampness between her thighs that she abandoned the real world and gave herself to my ministrations. That was how far reality stretched in Cuba—pretty far—and pretty good evidence of the politicization of life and of the body. Before getting into bed, I went into the bathroom to pee in the lidless toilet. A hose with a rusted, pierced tin-can lid was behind a shower curtain. There were two threadbare towels.

When I came back, Sylvia told me that she didn't feel well. Stretched naked on the rough sheet, she looked like a splendid cat, but the chicken at the Casa Grande terrace had unsettled her. She felt seasick. Instead of having sex I found myself comforting her as waves of nausea racked her, and as I drifted off to sleep I felt as if I were holding Cuba herself, battered by the sea. I woke up again and again, before light came through the curtain over the window. I was grateful for the morning. Night in the tropics is hotter than night elsewhere, and though the light of day was around us now, the night was still inside her, velvet dark, steaming and dense. "Ay, cojón!" she cried. "Aya, Dios mío!" And then, in a gentle tone of childish amazement, "Aya, Andrei!" My eyes still closed, I said "Ay, Cuba!" and meant it. I decided that Afro-Cuba was hotter inside and prettier outside than the rest of the Americas, and it made sense to me, in a torrid way, that Yankees went so crazy when they lost their *querida* Cuba. Temperature may indeed be destiny.

"What is," I asked her, "the secret of Cuban beauty? Cuban girls are so beautiful."

It was a stupid question, but the answer was real. My doctor said, "We eat very badly. There are no vitamins. We are beautiful because we are dying."

My whole macho world came to a grinding halt. I looked at her again, and saw that she had changed. Her body seemed evanescent, nearly transparent. Fashion-model skinny, she looked beautiful to my American eyes, accustomed to the death look of models and movie stars. There was frailty in her beauty, however, and something dimly perceived came back to me from our lovemaking. There was a lightness inside her that belied the dense fire. It was as if all her flesh had come together in her sex to provide the density. Outside the knotted root there was emptiness. Her beauty was an illusion, light feeding on lack, lack of vitamins, lack of protein. Her meat was thin, her bones hollow. I remembered the stringy flesh of a starving deer I'd once tasted in Pennsylvania: it had fed on nothing but grass and it was all sinew. But for all that, Sylvia's spirit shined, as if at the expense of her body. It must have taken an enormous effort of the will to gather enough flesh for my probing. Or enough hunger and lust together.

It was a horrific revelation. My doctor laughed: "We just want to dance," she said. "Girls just want to have fun."

We spent the morning in search of clothes, a form of payment acceptable to Sylvia's sensitivities. Her last night's dress was rumpled.

The dollar store for clothes was quite a distance away, and I had to purchase an airplane ticket for Havana. The ticket agency was crowded, with hundreds of people milling about in no apparent order while a few uniformed employees of Air Cubana ran dazed from desk to desk, struggling with malfunctioning computers. By the time I got my ticket, I had to meet my friends and get to the airport. I put a folded bill in Sylvia's hand and she stuck it in her purse without looking, her gaze steady on mine. "Will you write to me?" "Yes," I said, quite moved by the sincerity of the question. I wondered if she would be pleased to discover that the bill was one hundred dollars, five months' salary. Of course. Still, the sincerity nagged me and the vulgarity of the payoff made me feel guilty.

At the Santiago airport I met a German couple on their way to Varadero Beach. The leonine-maned, broad-faced man with his no-nonsense Frau held forth to me and to a shy Cuban bureaucrat with a bulging briefcase about his observations of Cuba. He delivered these in the stentorian voice of one used to being heeded. He reminded me of many similar Germans who roam Latin America in their khakis, self-consciously unconscious, bravely and ostentatiously frank, their well-traveled leather bags stickered with the name of every town. In Oaxaca, Mexico, I had met a couple in a Jeep with a big sticker up front that said, "Somos Alemanos!" Just in case someone might mistake them for *norteamericanos*. They believed that being German was an advantage somehow in the dark continents they "discovered" with grim liberality. They would have been surprised to learn that to the Mexicans who saw them, they were objects of humor because both their ideology and their shorts evinced embarrassingly pale skin.

The Santiago airport German centered most of his observations on skin color, to both my embarrassment and the Cuban's. He found "blacks" most interesting. Haitians, he said, are blacker than any other blacks, including Cubans. Haitians are blue-black, while Cubans are many varieties of chocolate, including white chocolate. The black Cuban cabdrivers ask only blacks for directions if they don't know where they are going. When you see lines forming at movie theaters the blacks all stand in their own line.

Listening to a middle-aged blond German say "blacks" over and over was genuinely creepy, particularly since the man believed that he was a friendly observer, a liberal through and through. It was as if he was programmed for racism and just couldn't help it. His wife, who sensed obscurely that Kurt might be putting his foot in his mouth, commented that the reason why they were so observant in these matters of skin color was that they had traveled everywhere and they had catalogued more natives than *National Geographic.* From the pit into the fire. Yes, the husband agreed, Germans are great travelers, they have a gift for observing people. Every nation has a gift. The Cubans, he was not afraid to say—he laughed with anticipatory delight—have a gift for lovemaking.

I took out my notebook. Such pearls should not pass unnoted. But before I could note anything, Kurt asked me blithely: "What is your origin?" I said: "My grandmother was Hungarian, my mother Romanian." But that, of course, wasn't the right answer. I should have said, "I am a Jew," which is the truth.

And at that point, a rolling wave passed under our seats and there was a drumroll under us. We swayed.

"That was an earthquake," said the shy Cuban, with some kind of grim satisfaction if not secret knowledge.

"Yes!" cried the German enthusiastically and, without a pause, "We experienced a 5.1 Richter in Guatemala."

Stop, I mentally begged him. The Cuban might feel that a larger earthquake was in order to silence this German.

Happily, the flight was called. I climbed into the heavy windowless AN-22 Soviet transport plane, grateful to be getting off the ground. A Swiss man took the seat next to me. I knew he was Swiss because I asked him if he was German, and he said: "No, I am Swiss." When we were airborne, plumes of white smoke started shooting out from under the luggage racks.

"We are on fire!" shouted the Swiss.

"It's not fire," I reassured the Swiss, "they just elected a new Pope."

His English wasn't too good, so he said that he was going to stay in Cuba to see the Pope. He thought that I'd asked him what he thought of the Pope, so he told me that he'd done his military service in the Vatican, guarding the Pope. That had been many years ago, under another Pope, so he very much looked forward to getting near this one. "There is sometink spezial on za Pope."

The miniskirted stewardess passed around a plateful of hard candy. All the Cubans were taking two. I only took one. The Swiss took three. I nodded out with the candy melting in my mouth and the Swiss reminiscing, but soon the stewardess poked me with her finger. When I looked up, startled, she had a paper cup with espresso in it. I took it and said: "How nice. In the U.S., they would never wake you up for coffee. They wouldn't even wake you up for lunch. In the U.S., sleep is more important than food and drink."

"Here it's the other way around," said the stewardess in perfect English, smiling.

DAY ELEVEN: PILGRIMAGE AND PENANCE

I didn't look forward to going back to Havana. Santiago had been an oasis. I didn't like thinking of the Capri lobby with its sour-faced policemen and the hordes of hungry *jineteros* in front. But there were some mitigating factors: Al Lewis in his cigar cloud, the beginning of the Havana Jazz Festival, and the San Lazaro Pilgrimage.

The San Lazaro Pilgrimage, a yearly event, was highly anticipated because of the Pope's imminent arrival. People from the far corners of the island walked for days to this shrine outside Havana to pray to San Lazaro, the patron saint of the sick, the infirm, the afflicted in body, heart, and soul. In Santería, St. Lazarus was represented leaning on a crutch and was the same as Babalu Aye. Images of St. Lazarus, emboldened by the Pope's proximity, had been sprouting on walls, in windows, and even on perches above the street. A hand-lettered sign said: "Chistmas is legal because San Lazaro blessed us."

We arrived in our hired car at the point where traffic became impassable. From here on, we were going to walk. The gritty suburb where we stopped unsettled our driver, who decided to stay with his car. "This is the kind of place they take your car, every piece." Just to make sure, he took the tire iron out of the trunk and stuck it in his belt.

Worshippers, singly and in groups, streamed from every direction, filling the hilly road. The late-afternoon sun was about to set in the hazy hills before us. It was approximately four kilometers to the shrine—not a great distance for us, but most of these folks had come from Havana and beyond. The pilgrims swayed, chanted, and sang. Some of them were holding lit candles, with one hand cupped around the flame to keep the slight breeze from extinguishing it. We fell behind the brood of a hefty older woman, holding a candle and telling a funny story to an adolescent girl who was laughing. A shy man and several children trailed behind them.

I asked her what she was going to ask the saint. She told me that she was going to see San Lazaro to thank him for her daughter's safe arrival in the United States, and to beg the saint to prod her girl to telephone or to write. Since reaching the United States seven months before, the daughter had given her family no sign of life. "We love her so much," the mother said. "Sometimes people go to America, they forget. They get new things, get married, never remember their house." A tear made its way down her round cheek. She put her hand over her heart, above the voluminous bosom pushing up her shapeless calico housedress. "You must never forget what is in your heart. Washing machines, telephones, those are nothing!" She started to cry hard now, and the young woman, probably her other daughter, looked at me reproachfully. She had been telling a funny story only moments before. I was sorry.

"I am sure," I said, "that San Lazaro will help. And the Papa is coming."

She agreed and her mood changed. "The Papa will make Cuba better. San Lazaro will make the phone ring." Her name was María García.

Her daughter explained that letters to and from Miami took three months to arrive, and that phoning the United States was too expensive. They had to wait for a call.

The sun set, and a thin velvety darkness streaked with gold and purple fell over the crowds. María García's mood changed again, and she began to sing a hymn in a beautiful, strong voice. She was joined by her daughter, and even by her shy son, who knew all the words. Other people joined in and the hymn picked up strength. I was amazed that so many people knew the words to it, that the memory of it had not been completely erased by decades of singing worker hymns and odes to the sugar crop. Musical memory must be the hardest to erase. Songs smolder at the bottom of the unconscious, always ready to flare. I remembered something, too: Felicia, a textile worker in my hometown in Romania, who told me in 1989, while sitting drunkenly on my lap that her brother, whom she loved more than anyone else in the world, had gone to Germany and hadn't contacted her in over three years. "Something must have happened to him," she cried, and then hugged me so hard with her strong worker's arms, I was out of breath. I thought that she believed somehow in her drunkenness that I was her brother, so I uncoiled her arms from around me and said, "He'll write you, I'm sure." "He promised to take me with him, he promised!" She was like a little girl, helpless. My heart was breaking for her, but I couldn't do anything. I didn't know her brother, I didn't live in Germany. I gave her twenty dollars.

The procession moved forward steadily, but here and there human swirls formed around a penitent. As night fell and we got closer, there were more and more swirls in the road. The penitents were crawling on their backs and knees to beg forgiveness and to punish themselves. A man inched along painfully on his back, with cinder blocks tied to his feet. He was dressed in a long, torn shirt and he contracted all his muscles like a wounded snake. Walking before him, another pilgrim swept the road with palm fronds. Propelling herself an inch at the time on her knees, a young woman made slow progress up the hill. Her knees were bleeding. Her mother swept the road before her with a palm frond. What kind of grievous sin could she have committed? The expression on her face was of an indescribable pain. Her eyes were turned upward. A legless boy in a flower-filled cart without wheels was being pulled up by his father. The ropes cut into the father's bare shoulders. Pilgrims surrounded the penitents and showered them with flowers and coins. In return, the bleeding penitents blessed them.

I asked the man coiling and uncoiling on his back with the cinder blocks tied to his feet what he was going to ask San Lazaro. His lips were dry, there was crusted spit in the corner of his mouth, he had only a few teeth, but in his left hand he clutched a bottle of rum from which he swigged.

"To help me to walk. My mom and dad brought me here when I was very young. They promised the saint that if I came each year I would get better a little. I've been coming since I was ten. I am forty now. Tomorrow I'll be forty-one. Do you have invalids in your country?"

I admitted that we had many invalids, and felt slightly ashamed sticking my shiny American microphone into the unshaven face of this emaciated wretch. I remembered how I'd expressed some squeamishness in Romania when my producer, Michael Sullivan—"Willy"—asked me to talk to a distraught widow. Willy had looked me over as if I were a jellyfish and said: "Yesterday I stuck my microphone into a grave." I didn't ask him what he hoped to hear from the dead, because I knew. People in Romania, especially mothers of the deceased, have the habit of throwing themselves into the grave. What Willy's mike was doing down there was picking up a mother's weeping. While I haven't become quite as tough as Willy, I know what the job consists of: bringing the grave to the world. Or the news of the grave, anyway.

I dropped some dollar bills in the bucket the penitent dragged behind him, tied to one of the cinder blocks. I realized that what he'd meant by asking me if we had invalids in my country was really qualitative, namely, "Do you have *such* invalids in your country? Such staunch believers? Such faithful, dedicated, insane masochists?" Yes, I supposed we did, but for the most part only the Church and communism have produced such totally perfect specimens. A group of believers gathered around and started chanting him to recovery. Or maybe they were chanting me away. I wasn't sure.

On the side of the road, dozens of shrines blazing with candles had sprouted into the night. Women sold candles and flowers. Every house along the road had become a shop, its doors wide open. The families sold sodas and sandwiches and displayed the best plaster saint they had, with candles blazing at its feet. There were also offerings of food and flowers and money. I bought six thin black tapers and a bouquet of tiny purple blooms to take to San Lazaro. I would ask the saint to forgive journalists. The most resplendent shrines rose baroquely seven or eight feet, and consisted of several sacred flower-and-fruit-laden figures. among whom I glimpsed, quite often, the waxy pale cheeks of the Bearded One and the intense gaze of Che the Holy Son. The figures had Santería bracelets and neck ornaments, a riot of colors that belied their immutable order. San Lazaro, leaning on a crutch, and a black Jesus predominated. Their Santería identities were either written on them or described by symbolic wreaths. A dozen shirtless men danced in a tight circle to the beat of seven drums. "They are going to dance all night," said the woman with the daughter in Miami. Their bodies glistened with sweat. The rhythm was complex.

Night fell and the stars pierced the sky like nails.

The altars by the side of the road vanished as we ascended the hill. There were no longer any houses, either. High chain-link fences now stretched on both sides of the road. At first, I only saw the dark shadows behind the fences, but then I heard them. It was a low murmur at first, then distinct voices. I lit one of my black candles and made my way closer to the side of the road. The shadows became faces. Hanging from the chain-link like clusters of grapes were young men. They were taunting the pilgrims with a monotonous chant. I listened. *"¡Ven acá! ¡Ven acá! ¡Bésame! ¡Bésame! ¡Te voy a mamar la pinga!"* ("Come here! Come here! Kiss me! Kiss me! I'll suck your cock!")

In response, the pilgrims sang their hymns louder. The taunting increased in intensity, too. On both sides of the road jammed with worshippers, the chain-link fences started vibrating. They were being pushed out. I was sure that any minute now, they were going to give and the mobs of young men would rush into us. In one section of the fence, standing on its own, was a silent family: mother, father, and two children. They stood apart, just looking; the young mother started mouthing the hymn.

"Don't worry about them!" a man said to me in English. "They give themselves AIDS on purpose to live there. They live better than us in the *sidatorio*. But don't go near the fence, because they cut themselves and rub blood on it so that you die if you touch it."

I had heard of the AIDS camps. Everyone in Cuba had been tested for HIV. Those who tested positive were interned in *sidatorios*, AIDS camps. Rumor had it that the inmates of *sidatorios* lived better than most Cubans. I heard also that people had purposely infected themselves to go live behind those wire fences, where the houses were, presumably, comfortable, and the food was plentiful. I also heard about women who shot themselves full of their lovers' blood to be with them in the camps. There had been an international outcry, and rules had been somewhat relaxed for the past two years. Inmates who could be trusted to behave were allowed to visit their families on the outside. The obvious benefit, or so the propaganda would have us believe, was that there was little HIV on the outside, making the island safe for sex tourism.

Art suggested that we talk to some of the men. David readied his camera. We approached the fence, but two security men sprang from the darkness. "Interviews are not permitted. Come back tomorrow. You can see everything then, talk to anybody you like." They pointed us to the middle of the road and we merged back into the mass, behind María García and her family. They were all singing very loud now, trying no doubt to drown out the voices behind the fences, and whatever other voices came threatening from the night.

The procession wound its way past the *sidatorio* and came up into the lights washing the Spanish church on the hill where San Lazaro worked his miracles. The church façade was lit from below, but the strongest lights by far were those of television crews, in particular CNN.

"There is techno-Santería here," said David. "Now there is a woman on her knees, coming toward me. With CNN right behind her."

The reporters had arrived ahead of us on a special road, driven in cars provided by the government. They hadn't walked at all and had missed the sweaty people, the hymns, the shrines, the penitents, and the *sidatorio*.

Inside the baroque church, worshippers moved on their knees to the statue of San Lazaro, which stood nearly buried in flowers and melted wax behind a mass of blazing candles. I deposited the blue bouquet there and lit a black candle and placed it among the others. I even mumbled an inarticulate prayer.

I sat down on a curb outside and wrote in my notebook. A blue-jeaned young woman approached and looked at my writing. "Are you a reporter?"

"Yes. Are you?"

To my surprise, she answered in the affirmative. Her name was Carmen and she worked for Cuban television. "News," she said, with visible sarcasm.

Art came up at this point, and I introduced them. She liked Art immediately and forgot all about me. "Did you ask San Lazaro for something?"

"Yes," Art said.

"Can you tell me?"

"I asked," Art said, "for better relations between Cuba and the United States."

At this, the young woman burst out laughing. It was contagious. I started laughing, too. Art was embarrassed. "What are you laughing for?"

Between peals of laughter, Carmen managed to say: "I don't know. People usually ask for something personal. Relations between Cuba . . ." She dissolved into laughter again.

"Well, why not?" said Art, annoyed this time.

I knew but couldn't quite explain it. Praying is a personal thing, but you have to be Christian to understand this. To a Catholic, praying for anything as abstract as "Cuba-U.S. relations" was quite incomprehensible. Art prayed like a Jewish liberal. Of course, I am Jewish, too, but I must be savvier, because I would never have told anyone what I'd prayed for.

"San Lazaro," I'd prayed, "give these beautiful, intelligent, talented, and starving people a break. Save us from cold wars, ideologies, and unreason."

Only kidding. But it wouldn't have been a bad prayer under the circumstances. It would have been okay save for the fact that the sports evangelist had said something nearly identical to the prostitute in his room at the Capri. And out loud, at that.

———

My relationship with my companions remained surprisingly warm after the whirlwind of the very long week now behind us. It seemed to me that we had gotten through many adventures. Mild teasing helped. David's willingness to play the gee-gosh innocent was an established part of the repertoire. I loved to hear him say, "I'd love a Snapple just about now," or, faced with a sorry street stand with five bottles of orangeade in it, "I guess this is the 7-Eleven." Or: "Where are the conveniences? How can people live without cars or public transportation? Gee." David's genuine though canny wonder became most useful when his eye, which missed little, fell upon someone he wanted to photograph. At that point, open-faced, American, with wonder-filled blue eyes, he walked right up to them and, with gestures unseen in Cuba for decades, charmed his subjects into compliance. David's "John Travolta thing," first discovered by Julie the *jinetera,* served him in good stead, too. Women jostled to get in front of his camera.

Art's embarrassingly sincere liberalism and easily swayed charitable emotions were also a source of amusement. At some leisurely interstice of afternoon in Lillian's *paladar,* a fly landed on Art's forehead and he hit himself hard trying to get it. Immediately, he said, "I'm sorry." "Sorry?" I asked him. "Sorry about what?" He wasn't sure. "I apologized to the fly, I think." "Maybe you apologized to yourself for hurting yourself?" I suggested. "I'm quite sure it was the fly," he said, not quite unconvinced. Then he fell into deep thought, trying to figure it out. I gave this matter some thought, too, and I now believe that Art really did apologize to the fly. He is the man about whom it was said that "he wouldn't hurt a fly." The original of that man, I believe.

I was very fond of our beautiful, ageless (thirty years old, really) ex–FMLN guerrilla guide and translator, Ariel Pena. There was, even in the midst of an emergency, a power of silent concentration in her. I associated her ability to become suddenly and deeply thoughtful with something Native American. When she fell silent she seemed to inhabit another place altogether, a remote and private space. At those times, her Indian features became more pronounced. She was astonishingly well-informed and accurate, but could become spontaneous and joyful in an instant. I particularly enjoyed her laughter, which was sudden, like the surge of a dolphin from a perfectly calm sea. I think that the greater part of our collective effort at wit and storytelling was intended to make Ariel laugh. Even when we almost thought of ourselves as a single organism, Ariel was both of us and not. Her mysterious past was a source of fascination, but her power resided in her character. I think that much of our Cuban journey was a performance for her sake.

She had a sense of drama all her own, too. One time in the car she was giving us a fine lecture on the sorry state of the Cuban economy, and then stopped to point out an arch inscribed "Socialismo o Muerte" just as we drove under it. That was timing. Ariel described other aspects of Cuba just as we passed relevantly sloganeered walls and huge portraits of Che. I never figured out if she timed her talks to end with visual illustrations, or whether the illustrations showed up spontaneously when she needed them. Once she parodied Fidel's gestures on television: "We are looking forward"—she pointed down with both hands—"to the future," with her hands behind her. That was physical shtick. Pretty good. Cubans were physically expressive and Ariel, though Salvadoran, had picked up some of their exuberance. (I was always surprised by people's sudden gestures. For instance, when Cubans want to tell you something important they pull the lower part of their eye down and say, "Mira!" Look at me. I always looked. It was scary. Or magnetic.)

Muchachos

Ariel Pena

DAY TWELVE: "RAVENS FOR THE FORKLIFT"

ORLANDO "EL DUQUE" HERNÁNDEZ

exquisite corpse no. 15

Ravens for the forklift.
The music tells us
where to burn
the black seeds
of our feelings.

—Ariel Pena, Art Silverman, David Graham, and Andrei Codrescu

There was a Christmas tree rigged with loudspeakers standing in the middle of a busy street in front of the Havana Psychiatric Hospital. It was blaring scratchy Christmas carols in Spanish. Behind the fence of the hospital, a row of inmates on wooden chairs was rocking back and forth watching baseball practice.

We were looking for "El Duque," Orlando Hernández, one of the greatest baseball players in the world, at the Havana Psychiatric Hospital where he was being punished by working every day as a physical therapy counselor. He had been banished from Cuban baseball for life for the crime his half-brother Livan had committed in defecting to the United States.

El Duque wasn't working, but it wasn't hard to find someone to help us locate him. An inmate on a bicycle led us through a maze of streets to his house in a modest Havana neighborhood. People nodded and greeted us as we passed, fully aware that these Yanks with microphones were on their way to meet their national hero. Most of them had not seen the World Series in which Livan Hernández had led the Florida Marlins to the championship; the game had been blacked out on orders from the Bearded One. But all of them knew that El Duque, their neighbor, was an even greater pitcher than Livan.

The Duke wasn't home, but his pretty young girlfriend, Noris Bosch, invited us to sit on the small front porch of their tiny house. She told us that she *had* seen the World Series with Orlando, thanks to friends from CNN who had smuggled them into the Habana Libre Hotel to watch on cable television. "Smuggled," because Cuban citizens aren't allowed inside tourist hotels in Cuba. Watching her calm and gracious manner, I wondered just how Cubans kept their wits about them in the insane asylum that was their country now.

El Duque came home shortly. A tall, handsome, self-possessed man, he emanated dignity and quiet strength.

We sat around the table in the one-room house and started talking. It became evident that this was no mere sports star, but a remarkable person raised on baseball and family love.

"It is a pleasure to shake your hand, because I know it's one of the best in the world."

"Thanks, but I'm just like any other person."

"How long did you play in the Cuban National League?"

"I played for ten years. I have the best pitching record in the history of Cuba."

"It's extraordinary to have two brothers who are great ballplayers."

"When I was a child, my dad taught me to play. He was in the minor leagues. When I went to bed, I had a ball, a bat, and a glove, instead of a toy. Livan and I played against each other, professionally, only once."

"You are both heroes in Cuba."

"I don't know. Many people thought that we were stars, but I don't think I'm the best. I want to be the only Orlando Hernández, that's all. I think Livan would have been great if he stayed here."

"He's not great now?" We were talking about the 1997 MVP.

Orlando smiled.

"How did you feel when he left?"

"I felt really bad. I knew I wouldn't see him for a long time. I wouldn't be able to help him polish his technique. I'm not there to help him."

"Have you been able to follow his career?"

Orlando began to answer, but Ariel sighed and her eyes filled with tears. Orlando looked as if he was choking up, too. His girlfriend, who sat on a chair next to him, wiped her eyes with a handkerchief.

"Sorry," said Ariel.

Orlando smiled at her, a beautiful full smile.

"I support Livan from here. I talk and give him advice, on the telephone. We are close. The only thing I can do is wish him happiness. Every one of his successes is mine. That makes me feel very, very happy. But I feel sad because I can't give what I know to the people of Cuba. I understand that I can't play. I have to pay for what my brother did."

"Seems unfair for you to pay for what your brother did. Even the Bible says that children shouldn't pay for the sins of their fathers."

"Well, there are two Bibles."

How could Castro's Bible be so cruel? It occurred to me that there was more than politics at work here. History might have been quite different if Fidel Castro, who had played baseball in the 1950s, had been drafted by the Major Leagues in the U.S. As rumor has it, he nearly was. Was the frustrated pitcher inside the dictator taking it out on El Duque?

"What was the sequence of events after his defection?"

"The first and hardest one is, I was suspended from baseball for life. Second, I cannot go out of the country and I can't represent Cuba as a player. It's a lot of humiliation. If there is something that keeps me alive, it's my belief in God. I was never interested in playing baseball for money."

"What are you doing with your time now?"

"I work now at the psychiatric hospital. It's a humane job. But it's not what I want to do. I get paid nine and a half dollars a month."

"You're not only a great player, but a great human being. Thank you."

"You don't know how much good this interview has done for me. This is what keeps me alive. Because if some people think that I don't exist, I just remember these moments. I come to realize that I'm alive."

Ariel could barely translate this. Her eyes were full of tears.

When we left, Orlando gave me his baseball cap, which he took off his head and inscribed "PARA ANDREI—El Duque Hernández, Habana, Cuba."

Four days later, on Christmas morning, Orlando, together with Noris Bosch and six others, hid aboard a fishing boat and trusted themselves to the sea. Many others had escaped Cuba the same way, but this group was not others. Orlando Hernández was a treasure, worth millions. He was also the first Cuban baseball player to escape in this perilous way. Others had just walked away from the team when playing outside Cuba.

DEFECTING CUBAN BASEBALL STAR
TO GO TO COSTA RICA

SAN JOSE, Jan. 7 (AFP)—Cuban pitching ace Orlando Hernández and seven other Cubans who defected last week will arrive here Wednesday from the Bahamas, a Costa Rican government official told AFP.

"It is very probable that Hernández and the others will arrive this afternoon on a private plane from the Bahamas," the source said.

Costa Rica's Migration Council approved visas for the defecting Cubans early Wednesday, the source said.

Hernández, nicknamed "El Duque" (the Duke), and the seven other Cubans were taken to the Bahamas after being rescued from a raft at sea on December 30.

On December 31 the U.S. State Department granted Hernández, his wife, and another baseball player, Alberto Hernández (no relation) permission to enter the United States.

Hernández has reportedly been weighing the U.S. asylum offer as part of baseball contract negotiations.

On Monday the U.S. State Department said Hernández would be given a "reasonable period of time" to decide whether he wants to come to the United States.

CUBAN BASEBALL STAR ARRIVES IN
COSTA RICA AND ASKS FOR ASYLUM

SAN JOSE, Jan. 8 (AFP)—Cuban baseball star Orlando Hernández and six other Cubans who defected last month arrived here from the Bahamas late Wednesday and requested political asylum.

"That's why we're here. In fact, we've already asked for it," Hernández said after he and the other athletes were seen getting off a private jet at Costa Rica's international airport at 23:15 p.m. (0515 GMT Thursday).

The group's arrival came as a surprise because hours earlier the Costa Rican consul in the Bahamas said Hernández and fellow baseball players were bound for Nicaragua.

"This is a dream come true. It's one of God's miracles. I lack words to express how incredible it all has been, because this is a great victory," Hernández told reporters.

The defectors were taken to the Bahamas after being rescued from a raft at sea on December 30. Their temporary permission to stay in the Bahamas ran out Wednesday.

On December 31, the U.S. State Department granted Orlando Hernández, his girlfriend Noris Bosch, and another baseball player, Alberto Hernández—no family relation—permission to enter the United States.

Orlando's sea journey was shrouded in mystery. Some of the newspaper reports mentioned rough seas and a leaky raft. Many twists and turns followed the group's rescue from a deserted Bahamian island. The famous Joe Cubas, agent to defecting Cuban talent, was on hand to manage Orlando's future. The United States offered asylum to Hernández, but not to the others. Orlando refused to go without them. Instead of coming to the United States, he went to Costa Rica; but this, of course, was a strategic move to gain baseball free agency.

The media fairy tale was filled, like all fairy tales, with perils and traps, false endings, and magical events, but it remained basically simple: after the perilous sea journey, the noble hero arrived in the United States, was reunited with his brother, and signed a $6.6 million contract with the Yankees. The Yankees! One can only imagine the fury of Fidel Castro, who has railed against Yankee imperialism for years.

Still, Orlando remained only another Cuban defector, whose prowess was unproven, until the night of June 3, 1998, when he stood on the mound at Yankee Stadium and pitched against the Tampa Bay Devil Rays. At the press conference that followed his indisputable triumph, he charmed the armies of the media with the same modesty and sincerity that had made him beguiling to the few reporters who had known him earlier. The Yankees didn't send him back to the minors, where he had been waiting for his chance.

But there is more to the story of El Duque. While waiting for the Call, he played for the Columbus, Ohio, Clippers, a triple-A farm team for the Yankees. I flew to Columbus on a sweltering May morning to renew our acquaintance, four months after we had met in Cuba.

Columbus sits in an all-American Midwestern landscape of corporate buildings, malls, and highways under construction. The city is booming. In its plainness, newness, car-driven culture, and lack of street life, Columbus is the antithesis of the peeling, crowded, throbbing, bicycle-filled, and very human city of Havana. The only thing they have in common is Columbus himself, who discovered Cuba; now, for a short time, they also shared El Duque.

The Clippers stadium was surrounded by bulldozers and cranes, which stirred up a fine red dust that made it hard to breathe. There was no escaping the sun on the hot bleachers looking onto the Astroturf. The Clippers were practicing: they had begun the season with the worst record in their history, 2–18, until the arrival of El Duque. Since then, they'd been practically unstoppable.

When I tried to clear time for an interview, a grumpy pitching coach said that Orlando didn't have any time. It was somewhat understandable. Journalists had been swarming and they cut into practice. Still, I felt that I had a special claim.

When Orlando was on his way back from the bullpen, I managed to get his attention. A big grin broke out on his face. We high-fived and I told him that I'd come to talk with him, but I could only stay in Columbus for one day. He said that he had a lunch appointment and that most of the day was taken, but that he needed to go shopping for clothes the next morning.

"Where, Orlando?"

"To the mall," he said.

And so it was that next morning, on another hot and windless day, I accompanied Cuba's greatest pitcher and new millionaire, Orlando "El Duque" Hernández, to a Columbus, Ohio, shopping mall that was physically and psychologically very far from the Havana Psychiatric Hospital.

Orlando drove his small rental car zestfully, singing along to a tape of Cuban salsa music, answering my questions and, simultaneously, talking on his elegant, palm-sized cell phone. During our next few hours together, he spoke on that phone about a dozen times, mostly with family and friends in Cuba, and about three times with Noris, who was in Miami. By the time we reached the mall, he had already expanded thousands of words into the world, near and far. He reminded me of a cheerful bird that can't contain its morning song.

This was not the man I had met in Havana. That one had been worried, sad, and under pressure. The new Orlando looked younger, acted younger, and seemed determined to enjoy himself. As a former refugee from a Communist paradise myself, I could sympathize. One becomes younger in America. Freedom is, among other things, cosmetic.

When I asked him if he would return to Cuba if the system changed, he said: "I will continue to play here. I am Cuban, I will always be Cuban. If things were normal, there wouldn't be any problem. Miami is closer to Cuba than Columbus."

That was a political irony that Orlando's little cell phone, with its distance-erasing ability, was trying to overcome. If the past was a land rich in personal significance, the present was a dazzling playground.

Orlando attacked the mall like a tiger. Our first stop was a shoe store. He stood among the bewildering varieties, studying their swirling shapes and colors, their wings, their panthers, and their wild-bird logos. He picked up a pair of Nikes and looked at them long and hard. There was something religious about it, as if the object weren't a mere shoe but the spirit of capitalism.

Orlando's taste in clothes ran to blue and black jeans and red T-shirts. In the clothing store, he headed for the jeans racks and tore through them as if they were Christmas presents. Wrappers flew everywhere. Like Nikes, denim was a totemic material to Cubans, just as it had been for Eastern Europeans. Not many years ago, in Bucharest and Moscow, one would be offered treasures for one's pants. For a time, denim was a currency in the communist world. Orlando still had about him the innocence of his country and, to him, these objects were Christmas presents. He had braved the seas on Christmas Day to get to them.

The original El Duque had been Orlando's father, renowned for his tastes in clothes and jewelry. Orlando had inherited the monicker, but he had a way to go before he equaled his father's pre-Revolutionary elegance.

"My first day in America we had a family reunion. Next day I went out with Livan and we had a very good time. He knows all the best places."

With packages safely in the trunk, we headed for the only Cuban restaurant in Columbus. The place turned out to be more Mexican than Cuban, and Orlando doesn't like anything spicy.

"I am a finicky eater," he said. "I didn't even eat conch on Anguilla Cay."

With that, El Duque told me the story of his escape from Cuba, in minute detail. The fishing boat he and his companions had been hiding in had reached the deserted Bahamian island of Anguilla Cay without incident. Rough seas had been predicted, and a storm raged on the Florida coast, but a "miraculous hand" smoothed the water in front of them. Their stay on the island was part camping adventure, part efficient labor division. Some fished, some prepared the conch, some made a shelter with branches. Their provisions had included bread, some Spam, and water. Orlando ate thin slices of bread and left the conch and the seaweed to the others. On the island, they found cooking utensils and the abandoned camps of Cuban defectors who had come before them. Twice, a reconnaissance plane flew overhead and they hid from it, fearing that it was from the Cuban air force. The first night they slept on the ground and watched the stars. On the second night it rained, and they took shelter, improvising a gas lamp from a piece of gauze and lighter fluid.

"It was bad when we ran out of Marlboros," Orlando said. "The captain's wife had some Cuban Populars, but I wouldn't smoke them."

El Duque Hernández will, no doubt, be the beloved hero of a fairy tale that will not stop before it is made into a major motion picture. (The Anaheim Angels had, in fact, offered a movie deal as part of their bid for Orlando.) He is uniquely a hero of our time, someone who defies tired political systems, crosses borders, is not afraid to upbraid a dictator. He is also supremely confident in his lucky star: the shine of it is in his eyes when he speaks. It has guided him, it has smoothed the waters, it has brought him riches and fame.

But this hero is hardly unidimensional. He is complex. Certainly, he is self-effacing, boyish, and heroic. He is thoughtful, though, when he advises other Cuban baseball players to think hard about escaping the way he did. "I didn't do it because I'm a hero," he said, "but because I'm crazy." What's more, this is a hero in the making. He has brought with him modesty and confidence, but he is now in the land of excess and temptation. How he deals with the overwhelming demands of our country, the flattery, and his own legend, will truly prove his mettle.

In Romania, the dictatorship collapsed shortly after the Olympian gymnast Nadia Comaneci defected to the West. There isn't an obvious connection, of course, but history isn't obvious and it does repeat itself. In any case, history has thrown Castro a wicked curveball.

EPILOGUE

AY, CUBA!

Attention is patterned by worldview. What you see when you look at anything, whether a person, a building, a city, or a country, is only a reflection—your worldview—coming back slightly colored. Alas. The best quality of an observer is empathy, which has to come with your worldview. No amount of immersion or adventure can take the place of empathy. If you look with love, you get back love. Ditto anger, indignation, or indifference. The Cubans are full of warmth, a vast reservoir of affection. To look at them with any other perspective is to miss them. In our thirteen days there, people opened their homes and hearts to us. In contrast to pre-1989 Romanians, they spoke openly. They were critical and warily dutiful about what they knew were the achievements of

Orlando "El Duque" Hernández and Noris Bosch

El Duque

the Revolution, though this particular kind of praise tended to take on slogan form. Mostly, they were ironic. They shrugged their shoulders and said, "Ay, Cuba!"—meaning "This is Cuba!"

"Ay, Cuba!" This was a cry of hopelessness and amusement, and the weary acknowledgment of a reality that made little sense. "Ay, Cuba!" What can one do? This is how absurd things are! But "Ay, Cuba!" was also an expression of pride: things don't make sense in a special *Cuban* way. And what is this *Cuban* way? Well, it is in part composed by the attention of the whole world riveted on the tiny island of Cuba. As far as anyone alive in Cuba remembers, the world has always paid attention to Cuba. This attention, whether negative, belligerent, or benevolent, is what makes Cubans stand taller, prouder. Cubans cannot imagine a day when the world will cease to pay attention, when it will become bored with little Cuba. That will be the day, then and only then, when life will not be worth living. Yes, things will be normal then, there may even be enough to eat, but life will be . . . unconvincing, pedestrian. Chalk up some of the current malaise of Eastern Europeans to this syndrome: the world has quit paying attention; we are alone, we are truly alone, we are marginal, we are stupid. The breath of the dead ideology gave us *presence*. What do we have now? Boring jobs, the rat race. We are no longer starving and elect. We are mediocre and small. When that time comes, "Ay, Cuba!" will no longer be heard.

The Pope proverbially came and went. In a weak voice, with the images of both Jesus and Che Guevara looking down on him, he urged Cubans to seek "new paths called for by these times of renewal." He filled the huge Plaza de la Revolución with curious but hardly worshipful Cubans, many of whom seemed pleased to see Fidel in a dapper suit sitting quietly through the homily. The religious images jostling the Revolutionary ones caused great hilarity. A man said, "The reason why El Comandante doesn't object to having Jesus next to him is because he thinks it's another picture of himself." The Pope called, as expected, for the end of the economic embargo. Fidel beamed. The Pope also called for clemency for political prisoners, and a few dissidents were released. In Santiago de Cuba, which *The New York Times* referred to as "the Rome of an Afro-Cuban faith," The Pope blessed Ochun, a.k.a. the Virgen de la Caridad del Cobre. In Santa Clara, before the Pope came, the local Communist Party served breakfast, including sweet snacks. It was a miracle. The Pope preached against abortion and birth control, but these themes fell on deaf ears. Cubans use abortion as birth control. The *santeros*, snubbed by the Pope, pointed out that their religion was better suited to help people endure present-day suffering. A man named Alberto Martínez said, "I love the Afro-Cuban religion because it cares for us now. The Catholics and evangelicals and others talk about the devil and inferno, but I want to deal with what's happening now."[41]

Within a month of my bittersweet visit, thousands of U.S. reporters descended on the island and began turning over every stone in search of stories. They wrote about taxis, cigars, hustlers, sex, the nearly extinct Jewish community, the music, the rituals of Santería, the crumbling architecture of Havana, the Baptist inroads on the island—millions of words that would have found their way into our minds and hearts, but for . . . Monica Lewinsky. At the height of media coverage of the Pope's visit, in the third week of January, 1998, the Monica Lewinsky story erupted and all the high-minded journalists of our best news organizations fled the island for what, in the end, really matters to Americans. If the Cubans felt that they had been given short shrift, they were right. One professional paranoid explained to me that "the Lewinsky story was released by the right wing to choke positive coverage of Cuba." But the opposite might also be true: a not-so-pretty picture could have emerged. Nonetheless, the mediatic hordes brought in dollars. Prices for hotel rooms and food quadrupled. Television stations paid the government a $100,000 "use fee" and the *jineteros* all bought new blue jeans.

The defection of El Duque Hernandez propelled our little group into the news. Since we were the last reporters to talk to him before his defection, our interview became the lead story on NPR and was picked up by CNN and the wire services. This was ironic, of course, because we didn't intend to bring back "hard" news, but rather a look at the daily lives and hopes of Cubans.

Many storms have battered the Malecón seawall since the days of the Venceremos Brigade, when young Americans, fired up with admiration for Che and Fidel, pledged themselves to the Revolution. Americans who come to Cuba now do so for different reasons, some romantic, some evangelical, some artistic, some business-related; and there are still some who love Cuba for its tarnished revolutionary ideals, for what it once stood for.

Everyone wants to know what will happen in Cuba, and when. The CIA has said that it sees no near-term threat to the staying power of President Fidel Castro. "Fidel Castro appears healthy for a man of 70, and his political position seems secure," CIA director George Tenet commented in a June 1997 assessment.[42] On February 21, 1998, the CIA released a scathing critique of its mistakes during the Bay of Pigs invasion.[43] Castro had been right, once again. There is your truth. Fidel is a rock now. He wasn't always, but years of power have hardened him. He is serene. He is negotiating with European capitalists, but in his heart of hearts he'd rather negotiate with Disney. Only Disney, you see, could keep Cuba both socialist and capitalist by declaring it Commieland, a place where the workers of the world can see the dream in action—and on vacation. Fidel will die a saint. *Ay, Cuba!*

Me: The End

NOTES

1. Heberto Padilla, *A Fountain, a House of Stone*. Translated by Alastair Reed and Alexander Coleman. New York: Farrar, Straus, Giroux, 1991.
2. Associated Press, Sept. 2, 1997.
3. Reuters, Sept. 24, 1997.
4. Hugh Thomas, *Cuba: The Pursuit of Freedom*. New York: Harper & Row, 1971.
5. Reuters, Sept. 9, 1997.
6. Jon Lee Anderson, *Che Guevara: A Revolutionary Life*. New York: Grove Press, 1997.
7. Ibid., pp. 544–45.
8. Margaret Randall, *Part of the Solution: Portrait of a Revolutionary*. New York: New Directions, 1973.
9. Margaret Randall, *Coming Home: Peace Without Complacency*. Albuquerque: West End Press, 1990.
10. Anderson, *Che Guevara*.
11. Randall, *Part of the Solution*.
12. Reinaldo Arenas, *Before Night Falls*. New York: Viking, 1993.
13. Ruth Behar, *Bridges to Cuba/Puentes a Cuba*. Ann Arbor: University of Michigan Press, 1998.
14. Himilce Novas, *Mangos, Bananas, and Coconuts: A Cuban Love Story*. Houston: Arte Publico Press, 1996.
15. *Paladares* are privately owned restaurants and hotels where tourists and Cubans can mix.
16. *Walt Whitman: The Complete Poems*. London: Penguin, 1975.
17. The Washington Senators tried out pitcher Fidel Castro in 1956 but didn't offer him a contract.
18. David Stanley, *Cuba: Travel Survival Kit*. Australia: Lonely Planet Guides, 1997.
19. François Rabelais, *Gargantua and Pantagruel*. Chicago: Encyclopaedia Britannica, 1982.
20. Stanley, *Cuba*.
21. Julio Hernández Max, *Obras Completas*. Mexico City: Goma, 1987.
22. Lawrence Ferlinghetti, *A Far Rockaway of the Heart*. San Francisco: City Lights Books, 1997.
23. *Cohoba* was the name of a psychedelic substance used by the now-extinct pre-Columbian Taino people. *Cohoba* made the world look upside down. A 1998 exhibit at the Museo del Barrio in New York displayed an array of curved spatulas with skull-and-serpent heads, carved out of skin, bone, and wood. They were used by the Taino shamans to stick down their

throats to make themselves vomit after ingesting *cohoba*. Can it be that Castro's Cohiba makes him see the world upside down?

24. Margaret Randall, *Cuban Women Now*. Toronto: The Women's Press, 1974.

25. Lois M. Smith and Alfred Padula, *Sex and Revolution: Women in Socialist Cuba*. New York: Oxford University Press, 1996.

26. Hudson Strode, *The Pageant of Cuba*. New York: Harroson Smith and Robert Haas, 1934.

27. Bernal Díaz de Castillo, *The Conquest of Mexico*. New York: Penguin Books, 1978.

28. Arenas, *Before Night Falls,* New York: Viking, 1993.

29. Thomas, *Cuba.* New York: Harper & Row, 1971.

30. Lewis Carroll, *The Hunting of the Snark*. New York: Penguin Classics, 1997.

31. Howard LaFranchi, *The Christian Science Monitor,* Nov. 7, 1997.

32. Ibid.

33. Richard Henry Dana, Jr., *To Cuba and Back,* 1859.

34. Larry Rohter, "Cuba's Unwanted Refugees: Squatters in Havana's Shantytowns," *The New York Times,* Oct. 20, 1997.

35. Lohania Aruca, "The Christobal Colon Cemetery in Havana," Translated by Narcisco G. Menocal and Edward Shaw. *Journal of Propaganda Arts no. 22,* 1994

36. William Lee Brent, *Long Time Gone*. New York: Basic Books, 1983.

37. James Dao, "Fugitive in Cuba Rubs a Wound in Trenton," *The New York Times*, May 1, 1998.

38. CNN, May 8, 1998.

39. Oscar Biner-Turman, "Virgen de la Caridad del Cobre." In *Larmas*. Buenos Aires: Pyramid, 1988.

40. Hayes Ferguson, "Marrying Foreigners Offers Cubans a Way Out," *New Orleans Times-Picayne,* April 26, 1998.

41. Juan Forero, "Santeria Faithful Feel Second-Class," *New Orleans Times-Picayne,* Jan. 24, 1998.

42. Reuters, Dec. 4, 1997.

43. Tim Weiner, "CIA Bares Own Bungling in Bay of Pigs Report," *The New York Times*, February 22, 1998.

ABOUT THE AUTHOR

Andrei Codrescu lived in socialist Romania until the age of nineteen. In 1989, after an absence of over a quarter of a century, he returned to cover the overthrow of the regime, and wrote *The Hole in the Flag*, a *New York Times* Notable Book of the Year (1991). His essays exploring questions surrounding the disintegration of communism have appeared in a number of his books, including *The Disappearance of the Outside* (1991), *Zombification* (1994), and *The Dog with the Chip in His Neck* (1996), the last two from St. Martin's Press. Mr. Codrescu is a commentator for National Public Radio, a professor of literature at Louisiana State University in Baton Rouge, and the founder of *Exquisite Corpse: A Journal of Books & Ideas.*

ABOUT THE PHOTOGRAPHER

David Graham is a documentary photographer with photographs in the collections of the Museum of Modern Art, New York, Art Institute of Chicago, and the Philadelphia Museum of Art. He has published two books, *American Beauty* (Aperture) and *Only in America* (Knopf). He also photographs regularly for *The New York Times Magazine, Time, Newsweek, Life,* and *Fortune.* Mr. Graham teaches at the Tyler School of Art. He is married to Jeannine Vannais and has two children, Dory and Xina. He grew up in the middle of middle America and his sister was chosen by CBS to be the "Typical Teenager" just to prove it.